CW00485831

A History of the Cathedral Church of All Saints Derby

Paul H. Bridges

Published by Derby Cathedral Enterprises Limited

2015

A History of the Cathedral Church of All Saints Derby

© Paul H. Bridges 2015   Dedicated to John and Elizabeth Bather

All rights reserved. No part of this publication may be reproduced, stored in a retrieval system or transmitted in any form, electronic, photocopying, recording or otherwise without the prior permission in writing of the copyright holders, nor be otherwise circulated in any form or binding or cover other than in which it is published and without a similar condition being imposed upon the subsequent publisher.

Published by Derby Cathedral Enterprises Limited

Printed by Moorleys Print & Publishing Ltd, 23 Park Road, Ilkeston, Derbyshire DE7 5DA
Tel: 0115 932 0643 ● Email: info@moorleys.co.uk ● Website: www.moorleys.co.uk

ISBN: 978-0-9931792-0-4

Left: A watercolour of *Irongate and the Church of All Saints Derby* by Louise Rayner (1832-1924). This view shows the south face of the late perpendicular gothic tower which was completed in 1532. The picture shows Irongate before street widening which commenced in 1866. The houses on the east [right] side of Irongate were replaced. The road widening process also removed the western border of the churchyard about 1871. Louise Rayner was born in Matlock, Derbyshire and brought up in London. She specialised in painting watercolours of old streets and passage ways in towns and cities.
© November 2014 Derby Museums Trust

Front cover: Detail from painting in oil by James Stephen Gresley (1829-1908). *A prospect of the town of Derby from Burton Road* circa 1861. The prominent tower of All Saints Church dominates the late summer scene. James Gresley was the first of three generations of artists from one Derbyshire family.
© November 2014 Derby Museums Trust

"The stranger who wanders through Derby in quest of objects worthy of remark, will find some defects, and more beauties; but when he arrives at All Saints, he arrives at the chief excellence – the pride of the place. It stands as a prince among subjects; a giant among dwarfs. Viewed at any distance, or in any attitude, the associated ideas of taste, grandeur, and beauty, fascinate the mind; the eye is captivated, and continually returns to its object, but never tires. Some pride, more sense and still more judgement must have combined in our forefathers in the construction of the noble tower; they wrought and we enjoy the credit of their labour."

From W Hutton (1791) The History of Derby

Contents

Preface

Over the years I must have walked past Derby Cathedral tower countless times. Usually I glance up and remind myself of its beauty; but recently it dawned on me that I had never really *looked* at it. If someone had asked me to describe the architecture and the decorative masonry, I would have been stumped. Perhaps I should draw the architectural features, I thought. Drawing makes one look, analyse, puzzle and ask questions. As I started to draw, the questions started stirring. The tower was built in the early 16th century but the ornamental moulding is fresh: so when was it restored? Was there a tower here before the tower we see today? What did All Saints Church look like in mediaeval times? When did All Saints first have a clock? How old are the bells? The list of questions grew but I struggled to find the answers. I realised that there must be others who have a deep affection for the Cathedral and would love to know more about its origins and its history.

The Dean of Derby, The Very Revd Dr John Davies DL very kindly allowed me to use the Rawlinson Library in the Cathedral Centre to research the historical background to the Cathedral. The book is structured so that you can decide whether to read the sections in sequence or to dive into the aspects which catch your interest. I have included a mix of photographs, engravings, drawings and schematic plans to help create a picture of the changing appearance of All Saints. I have not systematically described all the monuments and objects in the Cathedral. You will find such information in the Official Guide. The focus here is on the history of the Cathedral Church itself: the fabric, the people and the politics. The introduction presents a historical framework which is then developed in the following chapters. The final chapter includes a short summary and a chart of significant events from 917 through to 2014. I hope that you enjoy the book.

Acknowledgements

I am very grateful to John Davies for his encouragement and his close reading of the original manuscript. His corrections and thoughtful suggestions have resulted in many improvements. Jackie Croft (now Chapter Clerk and Administrator at Lincoln Cathedral), Lucille Parsisson and Kim Milner have been exceedingly helpful in enabling me to use the Rawlinson Library on many occasions. I am deeply grateful to Derek Limer, Keeper of the Treasures who generously gave me the benefit of his extensive knowledge of the history of Derby Cathedral and lent me valuable booklets from his collection. Maxwell Craven kindly provided information which improved my understanding of the foundation of All Saints Church in the new burh of Derby. John Armitage, Visitors Officer and Margaret Rhodes gave helpful information about the history of the interior of the Cathedral. Peter Hodgson and Roger Pegg, Trustees of the Bridge Chapel, very kindly discussed and sharpened my understanding of the history of the Chapel. Peter Hodgson also provided useful information on the pre-restoration photograph (Figure 9.4). I thank Lucy Bamford, Keeper of Fine Art and Matt Edwards, Curator of Visual Arts at Derby Museum for their help in obtaining permission to use four pictures. I also wish to thank the Bell Ringing Team on duty on 23rd August 2014 for the wonderful introduction and insight into the art of bell ringing. This helped inform Chapter 8. I am extremely grateful to Madeleine Bridges who gave valuable assistance in digitising a number of illustrations.

Sources of written information: This book has drawn heavily on a number of important written sources of information. These sources form the bibliography but key works must also be acknowledged here. *The Chronicles of the Collegiate Church of All Saints Derby* by Cox and Hope (1881) has been a major source of information. I must credit Maxwell Craven's excellent *Illustrated History of Derby* (2007) for deepening my understanding of contemporary events. Tomkins & Mallender (1973) provide a valuable account of the history of the organs and Halls & Dawson (1998) catalogue all the bells of Derbyshire. Dunkerley's (1988) beautiful book on the works of Robert Bakewell is especially highly recommended.

Sources of illustrations: I wish to thank the following organisations for kind permission to include illustrations for which they hold the copyright. Derby Museums Trust: the front cover, frontispiece and figures 3.4, 6.1 & 9.2; The Society for the Protection of Ancient Buildings: figure 9.4 from Armitage J, Glen D, Hodgson P & Nash H (2012). Other sources are as follows: figures 2.1, 3.1, 3.2, 3.6, 3.7, 3.8, 3.9, 6.2, 6.7, 6.8, 6.10, 6.12, 8.2 & table 8.1 are from Cox and Hope 1881; figures 5.1, 6.13 & 7.6 are from the *Derby Cathedral Guide* (1972); figure 6.3 is from *Life in Bygone Derby* (1977); figure 6.6 is from Tomkins and Mallender (1973); figures 7.2, 7.4, 8.1 and 10.1 are from the current Derby Cathedral Official Guide; figure 10.2 is a Cathedral greeting card; figure 7.1 and the photographs in the bibliography and index are from Eeles (1934). The other illustrations [marked PHB] are the work of the author.

1: Introduction

1.1 The aim of this book

The Cathedral Church of All Saints Derby belongs to the people of Derbyshire. It delights in their presence and participation in the regular services, the great Feast Days at Christmas and Easter and particularly the services to mark special occasions such as ordinations and the annual Bishop's Badge Service. The Cathedral also warmly welcomes the many visitors who come to see the fine architecture or to pray and reflect in the tranquillity within its walls.

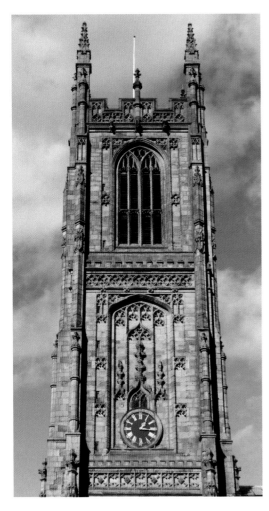

Figure 1.1: The south face of Derby Cathedral tower built in the late perpendicular gothic style by the Master Mason John Otes and completed in 1532. PHB

The Cathedral has its own committed and generous congregation but it aims to work with, and support, parishes and deaneries across the wider Diocese of Derby which stretches north to Chesterfield and beyond. All Saints is the Cathedral Church *of* Derbyshire and it is the Cathedral Church *for* Derbyshire.

Derby Cathedral has been a designated place of Christian worship for more than one thousand years. It was founded as a Collegiate Church and as a Saxon Royal Free Chapel towards the middle of the tenth century. Throughout the intervening centuries All Saints has served as a parish church but it has always played a wider role. At various times the church has held responsibilities greater than are normally associated with parish churches. During the 12th to 16th centuries All Saints was a major regional church which benefited from a fine mediaeval building, endowment with land and property, a college for clergy and large numbers of visitors from other parts of England and overseas.

During the early 16th century and the early 18th century the church was completely rebuilt in two phases juxtaposing two different styles of architecture. The first phase was the building of a very fine late perpendicular gothic style tower (Fig. 1.1). The second phase was the building of the main body of the church in a Roman Baroque style. The main body of the church was attached to the tower, built two centuries earlier, in an unpromising but ultimately successful marriage which has endured.

The church suffered serious losses including altars, statues, pictures and inscriptions during the mid-16th century Dissolution and it suffered again at the hands of the Puritans in the mid-17th century when windows were destroyed and the mediaeval font was removed. In the late 19th century, major reordering brought an increase in capacity but with the loss of much of a very fine wrought iron chancel screen. Happily this grille was progressively restored in 1905, 1927 and in 1972 when a major extension at the east end created much needed accommodation. All Saints Church was hallowed as a Cathedral in 1927 when the Diocese of Derby was created.

The aim of this book is to tell the story of All Saints Church from its inception to the present day. Using information drawn from a range of sources, this book provides an insight into the architecture, interior organisation and contents of the mediaeval church which existed before the construction of the buildings that we see today. As we will discover, there has not always been perfect harmony on matters relating to the church. These moments will be described too.

1.2 Early mediaeval disputes

The Collegiate Church of All Saints Derby was founded about 943 by King Edmund. From the outset it was designated as the *primary* church in Derby with a team of seven canons who were the senior clerics in an established College. It was also designated as a Royal Free Chapel which meant that it was independent of the episcopal control of the Diocese of Coventry and Lichfield. Early in the 12th century Henry I gifted All Saints Church to the Dean and Chapter of Lincoln Cathedral. This meant that All Saints was no longer independent but it was still a Royal Free Chapel outside the direct control of the Diocese.

This status was a source of on-going dispute between the bishops of the Diocese and the Dean of Lincoln who was also Dean of All Saints Church. The issue peaked in the 13th century. The Plantagenet kings had to remind the diocesan bishops that, much as they might wish to do so, they could not lever a parish share from All Saints. Income from All Saints was ultimately destined for the king. The story of this dispute is told in Chapter 2.

In the mid-13th century there was a serious dispute between the canons of All Saints and the Abbot at Darley Abbey regarding the lack of any payment in respect of the benefits which monks reaped from their activities at All Saints. This dispute was so intractable that All Saints referred the matter to the contemporary Pope who asked an archdeacon to arbitrate. This too is described in Chapter 2.

1.3 The mediaeval church

We have very little illustrative material on the mediaeval church which existed before the building of the gothic tower and the main body of the church that we see today. However, we have some glimpses in two engravings and there are many clues in the parish accounts and order books. In addition there are a number of items in the present church which were at one time contained in the mediaeval church. With detective work we can begin to piece together the architecture and the appearance and organisation of the interior. A description of the mediaeval church is presented in Chapter 3.

1.4 The Cathedral Tower

The Cathedral tower is a very fine example of late gothic architecture which has become the icon for Derby. It was built over a 22 year period from 1510 and we have some of the records of payment to the Master Mason John Otes. Chapter 4 focuses on the decorative architecture of this structure and gives some insight into the frequent need for repairs. The chapter also describes the spectacular 'flying' entertainment and the serious fire in the first half of the 18th century.

1.5 To repair or rebuild? That is the question

Early in the 18th century, there was a bitter dispute regarding the future of the mediaeval church building. The question was: should the once glorious but now decayed 14th century building be repaired? Or should the church be pulled down and replaced with a modern building? On one side the incumbent minister was keen to rebuild. On the other side the members of Derby Corporation and many parishioners wanted to restore the old church. Chapter 5 unfolds the story and explains just how bitter this dispute became. The tactics employed by the minister were extraordinary by any standards. The chapter also tells the equally intriguing story of his subsequent resignation.

1.6 The new church: the ever changing interior

A new church was built remarkably quickly [in just two years] to a restrained Roman Baroque design prepared by James Gibbs. The church was opened in November 1725 although the fund-raising continued for another five years. Chapter 6 looks at the interior architecture and shows how the positions of key features changed over the next 150 years to suit the taste of later generations. The chapter includes schematic plans to show how the pews changed and how the position of the chancel screen was frequently moved and reduced. Happily it was restored in the 20th century.

Figure 1.2: The chancel screen restored by Edwin Haslam (1905). This is the overthrow of the entrance gate to the Cavendish Area from the south aisle. PHB

We see lithographs of the attractive Prince Albert Memorial stained glass windows which formerly existed at the east end behind the altar. Chapter 6 also traces the story of the four organs which have occupied the central gallery since 1743.

1.7 The raising to Cathedral status

All Saints was selected to be the Cathedral Church for the new Diocese of Derby in 1927. Once again there were changes to the interior. In Chapter 7 we see the reversal of the Victorian attempts to beautify the church and observe the return to the original precepts of light and simplicity in the James Gibbs design.

Figure 1.3: View of the south face of the church showing the large windows of the south aisle alternating with pairs of Doric pilasters. The windows exhibit the Gibbs *surround* stonework. They are fitted with plain glass, which was restored in 1930 to give bright interior daytime lighting. PHB

1.8 The story of the bells and bell ringing

Derby Cathedral has the oldest ring of ten bells in the world. The oldest bell is the tenor (1520) and all the other bells were cast in the 17th century. Chapter 8 describes the inscriptions on the bells and illustrates some of the delightful artwork to be seen on the bells as recorded in rubbings taken by J Bailey. The chapter records some of the early peals performed at All Saints.

1.9 The Chapel of St Mary-on-the-Bridge

Derby Cathedral has had a long association with the Chapel of St Mary-on-the-Bridge which is one of the few remaining bridge chapels. In mediaeval times travellers would call in to the bridge chapel to pray for safe-keeping before embarking on their dangerous journeys.

Figure 1.4: The mediaeval Chapel of St Mary-on-the-Bridge [arrow] lies secluded behind luxuriant trees beside the river Derwent flowing under St Mary's Bridge built in 1794. Remains of an earlier bridge, of which the Bridge Chapel formed an integral part, can still be seen in the river. A four lane highway passes just to the south [left]. September 2014. PHB

With late 13th century origins, the chapel was probably built in the 14th century and formed an integral part of the mediaeval St Mary's Bridge. After its closure in the Dissolution, it was used as a residence and then a workshop and deteriorated rapidly in condition in the 19th century. The Bridge Chapel was restored in 1930/2 and it is now a place of regular Christian worship, closely linked to the life of the Cathedral. Chapter 9 tells that story.

1.10 Visitors to All Saints Derby

All Saints attracted high profile figures long before it was elevated to Cathedral status. The records show that Henry III came to All Saints in 1267. He took the opportunity, as was his right, to appoint a canon because there had been a vacancy for quite a long time. In the early 18th century Dr Henry Sacheverell gave a sermon which was so influential that some argue that it ultimately resulted in a change in government administration. Then in the mid-18th century, Bonnie Prince Charlie came for evening Holy Communion after his momentous decision to return north with his army to Scotland. These stories are told in Chapter 10.

A summary of the history of Derby Cathedral is presented in Chapter 11.

2: The origin of All Saints Church and the struggle for power and control

2.1 The origin as a Saxon Royal Free Chapel

All Saints Church was probably founded in the first half of the 10th century. In about 943, King Edmund 'illuminated' five midlands towns with the light of the Christian faith by establishing royal chapels in each one and it is believed that Derby was one of these five towns.

This fits quite well with our knowledge of the Anglo-Saxon origins of Derby. In a fierce battle in 917, the Mercian Queen Aethelflaed, sister of Edward the Elder, defeated the Vikings and re-conquered the area now called Derby. The Queen died in 918, but over the next 25 years, successive Anglo-Saxon kings - Edward the Elder, Aethelstan and Edmund, took control of Mercia and established a new burh called Derby. The royal territory was divided into long thin rent-generating burgage plots aligned perpendicular to a north-south axial road.

St Alkmund's Church already existed on the northern edge of the new burh. It had been founded in early Anglo-Saxon times, between 632 and 802 and was staffed by six canons. In establishing the new burh of Derby, it appears that a decision was taken to found a new centrally located minster to be dedicated to All Saints and served by seven canons - one more than St Alkmund's Church. Thus All Saints was probably intended to be the premier church in the new burh of Derby. This account of the origin of All Saints as a new minster in about 943 is consistent with the knowledge that devotions to St Edmund were offered at a dedicated shrine in All Saints Church during mediaeval times. The Domesday Book, compiled in 1086, provides confirmatory evidence of the high standing of All Saints Church in early Norman times. The original entry reads:

"En eodem burgo erat in dominio regis i aecclesia cum bii clericis qui tenebant ii carucates terre libere in Cestre. Erat et altera aecclesia regis similiter in qua bi clerici tenebant ix bobates terrae in Cornum et Detton similiter libere."

"*In the same town there was on the King's demesne one church with seven clerks who hold two carucates of land freely in* [Little] *Chester. There was too another church belonging to the King in similar fashion in which six clerks held nine bovates of land similarly freely in Cornum* [Quarndon] *and* [Little] *Detton* [Eaton]".

The King's demesne signifies his royal property and the church with seven clerks [canons] was without doubt All Saints. The other minster was St Alkmund's Church. The entry gives some insight into the area of the land possessed by each church but the units of measurement [carucate and bovate] were indirect and imprecise. One carucate was defined as the area of land which could be tilled by a plough drawn by a team of *eight* oxen in one year - about 100 to 150 acres. A bovate was defined as the land which could be tilled by *one* ox in one year - about 10 to 18 acres. All Saints Church was granted an estate of 294 acres at Little Chester, about half a mile north of present-day Chester Green. This may have been derived from a defeated Viking. Detton was probably a misspelling of Eaton.

Thus, All Saints Church (often called Allhallows Church with various spellings in 15th and 16th century accounts) originated as an independent Saxon Royal Free Chapel endowed with a significant holding of land at Little Chester. This royal status was confirmed by Henry I, Henry II, Henry III and Edward I. All Saints was also a collegiate chapel because the seven priests formed a College of canons.

Each canon was supported by a prebend, that is, a specified portion of church-owned property from which the income generated was used to support the livelihood of the canon. Hence the canons were prebendary priests. The canons lived in the College residence which was located on the north side of the Church grounds but the site was redeveloped in the 18th century and the building has not survived.

The descriptor 'Free' indicated that All Saints Church was not subject to the episcopal authority of the diocese. It was not required to make annual contributions to the Diocese of Coventry and Lichfield and the Bishop was not entitled to appoint clerics. This 'free' status became the source of tension between All Saints Church and successive bishops during the 13th century (see Section 2.4).

In summary, All Saints Church was probably founded by King Edmund as a Saxon Royal Free Chapel in about 943. It was a collegiate church with seven prebendary canons each supported by a specified portion of a large holding of land and property at Little Chester. As an independent 'free' chapel, All Saints Church was not subject to the authority of the diocesan bishop.

2.2 All Saints Church is gifted to Lincoln

Very early in the 12th century, probably between 1100 and 1107, All Saints lost its independence. Henry I gifted All Saints Church together with the churches at Ashbourne, Wirksworth and Chesterfield, to the Cathedral Church of St Mary in Lincoln. As a consequence, the Dean of Lincoln took the title of Dean of the Collegiate Church of All Saints Derby. About 60 years later, between 1161 and 1170, Hugo of Derby founded an Abbey at Darley and was styled 'Dean of Derby'. Subsequently Henry and Robert of Derby also held the title 'Dean of Derby' and the title continued to be used well into 13th century.

There is uncertainty as to whether these clerics were sub-deans of All Saints Church appointed by the Dean of Lincoln or were priests at St Alkmund's Church who became abbots of the Abbey at Darley. Since the Dean of Lincoln also held the title of Dean of the Collegiate Church of All Saints, it seems more likely that these deans were clerics at St Alkmund's Church. The title 'Dean of Derby' fell out of use in the mid-13th century but it was re-introduced at the end of the 20th century, when new cathedrals which had previously been parish churches were permitted to title the most senior cleric *dean* rather than *provost*. In 1999, the style of 'Dean of Derby' was reinstated after a break of about 800 years.

In the 13th century, All Saints was similar to a small cathedral with seven priests who were equivalent to cathedral canons, but the Diocese of Coventry and Lichfield in the region was not empowered to exercise episcopal authority. The Dean of Lincoln had the responsibility and authority to appoint the sub-dean and the other prebendary priests [canons] to administer affairs at All Saints. However, since All Saints Church was a *Royal Chapel*, the King also had the right to make appointments at All Saints; and on one occasion he did. On Easter Day 1267, Henry III visited All Saints Church and discovered that there was a long-standing vacancy for a canon. He appointed a chaplain by the name of Roger to the position and informed the Dean of Lincoln accordingly.

The Dean of Lincoln received annual payments from All Saints Church which contributed to his very considerable income. So for the period from the beginning of the 12th century to the Dissolution of the College at All Saints Church in 1549, in the reign of Edward VI, the most senior priest at All Saints Church Derby was the sub-dean who was responsible to the Dean of Lincoln.

2.3. The dispute with Darley Abbey

In 1252 a bitter dispute arose between the monks of the Abbey at Darley and the prebendary canons of All Saints. The canons claimed that the monks of the Abbey entered All Saints at various times and would celebrate mass, hear confessions, receive penances, administer blessed bread and anoint the sick. Yet despite benefiting from these services, they refused to pay a tithe to All Saints as requested by the canons. When the canons of All Saints felt that they could not reach a resolution, the matter was referred to Pope Innocent IV. The Pope, who may have had more pressing concerns, issued a Bull in Milan in September 1252, appointing Giles, Archdeacon of Berkshire as arbitrator.

Archdeacon Giles gave his decision at the Cathedral of St Frideswide at Oxford, one day after the feast of St John-at-the-Latin-Gate 1253. The boundaries of the parishes of All Saints and St Alkmund's were coterminous with the royal demesne and the Abbey at Darley had been built *within* the limits. The Archdeacon found firmly against the Abbey and determined that they should pay not less than one mark and not more than two marks each year. One mark equated to thirteen shillings and four pence (13s 4d or 160d) which was two thirds of one pound [240d]. Since one penny corresponded broadly to one day's wage for a manual labourer, perhaps around £50 today, the annual tithe due from Darley Abbey would have been equivalent to about £8,000 to £16,000 today. In addition, Archdeacon Giles also charged the Abbey twenty shillings (20/-) (£1) for the cost of the arbitration. This would be about £12,000 today. So the priests of All Saints were vindicated and it was quite an expensive settlement for Darley Abbey.

2.4 Bishops attempt to exert episcopal control

We recall that authority over All Saints Church was vested in the Dean of Lincoln at the beginning of the 12th century. Through much of the 13th century, successive bishops and archdeacons of the Diocese of Coventry and Lichfield attempted to exercise authority over All Saints Church and levy contributions similar to the parish share of today. In 1254, Henry III warned Roger de Wexeham, the Bishop of Coventry and Lichfield that he was not to collect tithes from All Saints because the church was a Royal Free Chapel exempted from ordinary episcopal control. The King told the Bishop that he had appointed receivers with the assent of the Papal Legate Adrian, Cardinal Deacon. All Saints would pay the annual sum of six marks [£4] to the Treasury through the offices of the Dean of Lincoln. Roger de Wexeham had formerly served as the Dean of Lincoln between 1239 and 1245, and it is possible that he was attempting to retain his influence over All Saints.

In 1275, Edward I exempted All Saints from making a payment of 50s 8d (£2.53p) to Roger Longespée, Bishop of Coventry and Lichfield. However, All Saints was expected to make a contribution to the Treasury. The Church paid six marks (£4) annually into the Treasury through the Dean of Lincoln. Edward I reaffirmed All Saints Church as a Royal Free Chapel in 1278 subject to the direct authority of the Pope (Fig. 2.1).

Figure 2.1: The Common Seal dating from the reign of Edward I (1272-1307) signifying the status of All Saints Church in Derby as a Royal Free Chapel. From Cox & Hope (1881).

Undeterred by previous events, Bishop Roger Longespée continued his attempts to extract tithes from All Saints Church in the following years. So at Michaelmas 1285, he was summoned to the King's Court Winchester accused of contempt of the King *and the See of St Peter*. The representative of the Bishop argued that diocesan bishops had always enjoyed certain rights at All Saints, as for example Bishop Alexander Stavely (1224-

1240) apparently had done. The Dean of Lincoln countered that All Saints had from time immemorial been free of ordinary jurisdiction and since <u>he</u> had responsibility for the appointment of the prebendary priests, he rather than the Bishop had the right to make visitations to All Saints.

The Court concluded that both sides had made a substantive case. The Dean of Lincoln had the authority to appoint the sub-dean and canons without input from the bishop; and he also had the right to receive annual payment. While the Bishop of Coventry and Lichfield had no right to demand contributions to the Diocese, he did have the right to conduct services of ordination, hold synodals and exercise discipline over clergy, chaplains and parishioners at All Saints Church.

This did not entirely settle the matter; neither the King nor the Bishop felt content. On 27th September 1288 the King sent a letter to Bishop Roger Longespeé prohibiting any interference with All Saints Church; there should be no *visitations*. In 1292, as further clarification, the King informed the Bishop that he [the Bishop] did <u>not</u> hold the powers as Visitor to free chapels in the diocese. Therefore, there is no reference to All Saints in the episcopal register at Lichfield – but bishops of Coventry and Lichfield were permitted to hold ordinations.

Indeed, at the beginning of the 14th century, large ordination services were held at All Saints Church. These were conducted in the name of Walter de Langton, the Bishop of Coventry and Lichfield by John Halton, Bishop of Carlisle, who often acted as suffragan [assistant]. This arrangement arose because incursions into the English borderland from Scotland made life too dangerous to administer the northern diocese from centres in the vicinity. So the Bishop of Carlisle located his palace at Melbourne in Derbyshire where he could conduct his diocesan business in peace.

It would appear that in return for this facility, Bishop Halton was prepared to assist Bishop Langton by presiding at major ordination events conducted at All Saints Church. In 1301, Bishop Halton ordained 64 men as sub-deacons (22), deacons (9) and priests (33) in the name of Bishop Langton. The following year he conducted a further 139 ordinations at All Saints.

3: The mediaeval church

3.1 The appearance of the mediaeval church

The earliest part of the building which now constitutes the Cathedral Church of All Saints is the tower which was built in the late perpendicular gothic style and completed in 1532. The rebuilt main body of the Cathedral was constructed nearly two centuries later in 1725, with an easterly extension completed in 1972. Some of the contents of the Cathedral, for example the c. 1520 tenor bell, the 15th century alabaster slab dedicated to Sub-Dean John Lawe and the monument to Bess of Hardwick (1608), pre-date the stonework which now contains them. All Saints existed as a church for nearly 600 years before the construction of the current tower, so what did the earlier, mediaeval, church look like? Do we have any clues?

We know from records that there was significant building work in the 14th century but we do not know if this was substantial repair of an earlier building or a major rebuild. There are only two pictures which give a glimpse of the post-14th century building. The first is a small copper plate engraving (or etching) which is labelled 'Derby Church' (Fig.3.1). The second is a fine engraving of the prospect of All Saints and the surrounding buildings viewed from the east drawn by an unknown artist c.1690. In addition, there is also a large-scale map of the vicinity of All Saints which shows some detail of the church, dated 1599. We shall consider first the engraving of Derby Church, then the map (1599) and finally the east prospect (1690).

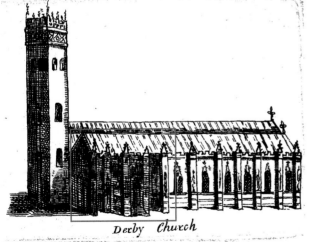

Figure 3.1: Derby Church viewed from south. This engraving shows the 14th century body of the church attached to a tall slim tower. Is this the predecessor to the present tower? The red box delineates the South Porch which is enlarged in Figure 3.2. The engraver is not known. From Cox & Hope (1881).

In their Chronicles, Cox and Hope regarded the small engraving of Derby Church as mid-17th century in age. It was presumably prepared from a contemporary or earlier drawing, now lost. The engraving shows the church viewed from the south. If the mid-17th century date of the engraving is correct, it should depict the 16th century rebuilt tower attached to the mediaeval church building. Indeed the church building is very clearly the mediaeval structure. The main body of the church featured a series of six alternating windows and buttresses. Each window had three lights: one quatrefoil single light window above a pair of lights separated by a mullion. Each light had a trefoil head. The buttresses were surmounted by pinnacles decorated with crockets and capped by finials. There was a prominent and very fine South Porch which had two side windows and a large South Door. The parapet of the south wall was battlemented.

Figure 3.2: An enlargement of part of Figure 3.1 to show more detail of the South Porch. Note the buttresses [B] with pinnacles [P] and crockets [C]. The South Door appears to have steps [S].

The tower shown in the Derby Church engraving is curious. It resembles the current tower in that it is tall with elegant pinnacles. However, there are several important differences between the tower in the picture and the tower that we see today. First, the tower in the picture appears more uniform in width and slender than the current tower which reduces in cross-sectional area through three successive stages. The tower in the picture has no buttresses whereas the current tower has two angle buttresses in each corner, giving a total of eight buttresses which continue to the top of the tower. The picture shows no west door to the tower, yet the West Door of the tower has been a major entrance to the Cathedral since 1532. The highest stage shows a pair of windows on each side while the current tower just has a single louvre window on each side of the bell chamber. There is no clock face on the west side of the tower in the engraving, yet we know that in the 16th century, there was a clock face positioned just below the level of the West Window. It was moved to a higher position in the 18th century.

Some authors have dismissed these differences as omissions and errors in the preparation of the engraving. Certainly the engraving lacks precision. Only the pinnacles of the tower appear to be 'correct'. If the suggested 17th century date for the engraving is correct then one would expect it to be based upon a contemporary picture in which case this picture suffered from omissions and significant inaccuracies. However, is it possible that the original picture was drawn in the 15th century and the engraving actually shows the complete mediaeval church *before* the rebuilding of the tower in the early 16th century? There was certainly an earlier west tower because there are records of re-pointing the stonework of this mediaeval tower in 1475. The mediaeval tower probably pre-dated the 14th century re-building episode and would therefore have been in a poor physical state by the end of the 15th century. It collapsed or was pulled down some time before 1509.

Let us consider each of the noted differences in turn. Firstly, did the artist of the original drawing or the engraver, neglect to draw the important West Door to the tower which is now the principal entrance to the church or is the engraver correct in showing the mediaeval tower without a west door? The principal entrance to the mediaeval church, indicated by the engraving, was through a large South Porch. The absence of a west entrance would of course have made a south entrance a necessity. Secondly, did the artist or the engraver, omit the prominent buttresses on each corner of the tower and the progressive reduction in cross-sectional area of the 16th century tower or does the engraving show an earlier mediaeval tower which lacked buttresses? Thirdly, did the artist or engraver, wrongly show two windows on each side of the highest stage of the 16th century tower when there was actually only one large window on each side of the bell chamber or is this a correct representation of the mediaeval tower? Finally, did the artist or engraver, omit the clock dial on the west face of the 16th century tower in error or is this a representation of the mediaeval tower which did not have a clock?

From this analysis, it is concluded that while the engraving may show the 16th century tower and the mediaeval body of the church as suggested by previous authors, the extent of the differences between the details shown in the engraving and the architectural details of the 16th century tower are considerable. One would have to argue that important details relating to the tower were omitted or fabricated. It is suggested here that the engraving is a fair representation of the mediaeval tower and body of All Saints Church as it appeared in the 15th century, before the rebuilding of the 16th and 18th centuries.

The map (1599) depicts the ground plan of the mediaeval church (Fig. 3.3). It shows a wide south aisle, a wide nave and a narrow north aisle all of the same length. The nave passes eastwards into the quire which in turn leads eastwards into a rob-easy or re-vestry. To the south of the quire and in continuation with the south aisle is St Katharine's Quire. The easterly projecting re-vestry is curious because it is not in evidence in either of the two engravings. Both engravings seem to show the east wall as straight.

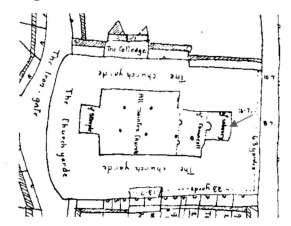

Figure 3.3: Map of All Saints Church area c.1599. The eastward projecting re-vestry [arrow] is not consistent with the two engravings. Note the short narrow north aisle and absence of the south porch which surely was an omission. Note the wide frontage to the west of the Church and The College to the north of the Church. From Mallender 1977.

The ground plan therefore shows the east end of the mediaeval church as irregular in shape with the rob-easy projecting eastwards. There is no sign of this projecting structure in the engraving of c.1690 (Fig. 3.4) which views the church from some distance. We should note that there was substantial rebuilding of the gable end of the mediaeval church in 1676 and so we should not be surprised if the engraving of 1690 does not match the ground plan of 1599. Perhaps the vestry was relocated to the north of the chancel before 1690.

12

Figure 3.4: Part of an engraving showing All Saints Church and the surrounding buildings viewed from the east. The engraving was made from a painting by an unknown artist about 1690 which was after major repairs in 1676 but before the rebuilding in 1723-5. Two large decorative style east windows are visible [arrows]. These are probably the window of St Katharine's Quire [left] and the window behind the High Altar [right]. © November 2014 Derby Museums.

The second picture is a fine quality engraving of the prospect of Derby viewed across the river Derwent from the east (Fig. 3.4). The engraving dates from about 1690 and shows the mediaeval church of All Saints before the rebuilding of 1723-5. It therefore post dates the ground plan by about one hundred years. The picture clearly shows twin east-west aligned gable roofs spanning the main body of the church. The southern gable covered the wide south aisle and St Katharine's Quire. The northern gable covered the nave, quire and north aisle. Cox and Hope (1881) suggested that the narrower north aisle was covered by a lean-to roof which joined onto the northern gable.

The mediaeval church was richly endowed with six altars and numerous shrines. In addition to the High Altar, there were altars dedicated to Our Lady, St Katharine, St Nicholas, the Holy Trinity and the Passion. In addition there were shrines to The Rood, Our Lady of Pity, St Christopher, St Clement, St Edmund [the founder], St Eloy, St George and John the Baptist. The sub-dean and his team of canons would have been supported by chaplains and deacons in the task of celebrating mass at the chapel altars each day.

During the reign of Edward VI, the bailiffs and burgesses of Derby Borough ordered that mass should be provided at the Altar of the Holy

Trinity in the Chapel of the Trinity Guild at 5 am each day to pray for the brothers and sisters of the Guild and the safe-keeping of travellers and parishioners. This facility may have become necessary after 1547 when the Chapel of St Mary-on-the-Bridge was closed.

In their Chronicles of the Collegiate Church of All Saints, Cox and Hope (1881) drew upon their experience to suggest the most likely positions for the altars. These have been mapped onto a schematic plan of the mediaeval church (Fig. 3.5).

The Mediaeval Church - circa 1500

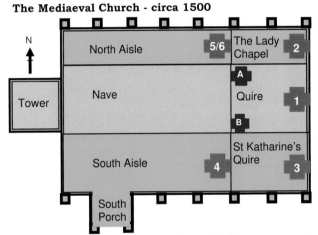

Figure 3.5: A schematic plan of the mediaeval church showing the positions of the altars suggested by Cox and Hope (1881). The altars are: 1 – The High Altar; 2 – Our Lady; 3 – St Katharine; 4 – St Nicholas; 5 – Holy Trinity; 6 – The Passion. A – The Shrine to the Rood and B – The Shrine to Our Lady of Pity. Note the narrow north aisle and the buttresses around the perimeter of the building. PHB

The seating in the mediaeval church would probably have been in the form of long benches with low backs and open ends. Box pews were not introduced until the early 17th century.

3.2 The importance of All Saints Church

The Collegiate Church of All Saints of the middle ages was a church of considerable importance. It was well endowed with extensive prebendary land and property at Little Chester which supported the sub-dean and his team of six fellow canons. In addition the church had gained substantial pasture, arable land and properties in south Derby, so there was a significant annual rental income. As a Royal Chapel with formal connections to Lincoln Cathedral, All Saints attracted visitors from across the country and from overseas. The visitors would have been a further source of income. The church must have had a splendid and impressive interior with the six altars, eight shrines dedicated to saints and the many statues and pictures. Amongst the shrines, one was dedicated to St Edmund the founder of the church circa 943. This rich heritage perhaps explains how All Saints was able to attract the funding for the construction of an elegant tower early in the 16th century before the losses of the Dissolution and the destruction wrought by the Puritans during the 17th century.

3.3 Memorials to two sub-deans at All Saints

Two memorial pieces to sub-deans who held high office as the most senior clerics in Derby in the 15th and 16th centuries, have survived the subsequent Dissolution, the Puritan purge and the rebuilding of the church.

Figure 3.6: An alabaster slab inscribed with the image of Sub-Dean John Lawe, senior cleric during the mid 15th century. From Cox & Hope 1881.

The first is an alabaster slab which has an inscribed image of Sub-Dean John Lawe who was known to be active around 1440 (Fig. 3.6). He is shown in the vestments of a canon holding the communion chalice. He is surrounded by gothic ornamental masonry. Is

it possible that we are gaining some insight into the masonry that decorated the entrance porch as Sub-Dean Lawe welcomes the faithful to All Saints?

The second memorial piece is a large effigy of a sub-dean thought to be Sub-Dean Robert Johnson who was active around 1527 (Fig. 3.7).

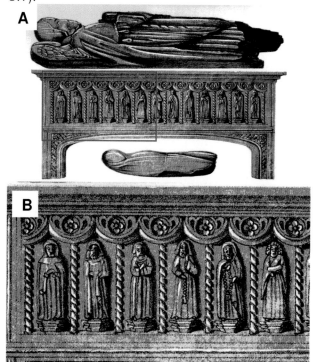

Figure 3.7:
A. An effigy of Sub-Dean Robert Johnson carved in wood. Johnson was Sub-Dean at All Saints about 1527 when the tower was almost complete.
B. A close up of the bedesmen on the panel below the effigy. This lithograph was made c. 1881 after the first restoration but before the recent addition of the watchful dog. From Cox & Hope (1881).

The effigy is carved into wood and he is shown with his head resting on a pillow held by two angels. A [newly carved] dog sits at his feet alert and protecting his master. There is a second effigy of a wrapped cadaver at the base of the monument. Carvings of thirteen figures are shown on the front panel below the main effigy. These were beneficiaries of the charity founded by Robert Johnson and were expected to pray that his soul should pass without delay from purgatory to Heaven. This splendid monument only just survived. After the demolition of the mediaeval church, the panel was located on the east wall of the new church but the effigy was consigned to the damp town vault where it languished - slowly decaying for 157 years until it was rescued and restored in 1880. It was restored again in 2010.

3.4 The annual income of the churches

The physical estates of All Saints and St Alkmund's churches were merged during the reign of Henry III. The seven canons in All Saints Church and the six in St Alkmund's Church were replaced by a team of seven canons to service both churches. In 1269 the annual income of All Saints Church was returned as 60 marks (£40) (about £400,000 today). Twenty two years later in 1291 the Taxation Roll of Pope Nicholas IV stated the annual income to be £25 6s 8d and the annual rental income from lands at Little Chester, Little Eaton and Quarndon was shown as £17 7s 1d. In 1329 when Anthony Beck was Dean of Lincoln, the annual income from the property at Little Chester, Little Eaton and Quarndon had increased to £30 7s 1d (about £250,000 today).

In *Valor Ecclesiasticus* [early 16th century], it is recorded that the annual income raised by All Saints was £38 14s 0d. We recall that in 1253, Archdeacon Giles had determined that Darley Abbey should make an annual payment to All Saints Church of between one and two marks (13s 4d to 26s 8d) (Chapter 2.3). Two hundred years later in the mid-15th century, this arrangement was reaffirmed by an agreement reached by Roger Newton, the Abbot, and John Lawe, the Sub-Dean at All Saints. During the early 16th century, before the Dissolution, Darley Abbey paid the sub-dean of Derby an annual sum of £11 (about £35,000 today).

In the 14th century the Dean of Lincoln lost the right to receive the payments through what appears to have been an act of humanity. The Dean of Lincoln was required to hear cases of alleged transgressions of the law brought to the manorial court. He decided to impose *fines* upon bakers and brewers who were found guilty of breaking the regulations on the fixing of prices on bread and beer. The prescribed punishment for these offences was either the pillory or the tumbrel. The latter was a particularly unpleasant and potentially life-threatening punishment whereby the offender was tied to a cucking-stool and then completely immersed in foul water. By imposing mere fines instead of the pillory or tumbrel, the Dean had infringed the rules of the Royal Court and he was required to forfeit his right to receive payment from the Royal Chapel at All Saints.

3.5   The Dissolution and the subsequent intervention by Queen Mary

The implementation of the Dissolution of the monasteries and Reformation of the churches proceeded in two phases. The first phase involved institutions with an annual income of less than £200. St Mary's Church with a monastery at Burton was one of three Derby churches which had a total annual income of about £40. The second phase involving institutions with an annual income of more than £200 began in 1538. This phase involved the Abbey at Darley which had an income of £258 13s 5d. All Saints Church was not included because although it was collegiate, it served a parish community. However, when the young Edward VI came to the throne in 1547, Lord Somerset became 'Protector' and he adopted a more extreme position. The physical estate of the churches of All Saints and St Alkmund's was sold for £346 13s 4d which would equate to between £1 million and £1.2 million today. At a stroke, the churches were stripped of the resources used to maintain the church buildings and pay the stipends of the seven canons. This left All Saints Church unable to provide for the spiritual and pastoral needs of the faithful in the parish.

Fortunately for All Saints, Queen Mary was prepared to make an intervention which would address the major problem. In 1555 Queen Mary made a large grant of the former church land and property confiscated by Edward VI to the bailiffs and burgesses of the Derby Corporation. This gift was granted on condition that Derby Corporation should appoint two priests to officiate at All Saints Church and that they should each be provided with a vicarage and an annuity of £7 6s 8d. All tithes of corn, hay, wool and lamb under the tenure of Richard Corton of Quarndon were given to the town. In the following years, there were ongoing disputes between the farmers of Quarndon and the Church Wardens of All Saints as to what proportion of the cost of repairs to the church the farmers should bear. Finally, in 1620 it was decided that Quarndon farmers would pay one-tenth of the annual assessment.

3.6   Joan Waste: 16th century martyr

The divide between Protestantism and Roman Catholicism became painfully evident during the reign of Queen Mary who came to the throne after the death of the young King Edward VI in 1553. During her reign people were expected to follow Catholic doctrine. A young woman aged 22 called Joan Waste had been blind from birth and was a committed and forthright Protestant. She attended All Saints Church regularly where parishioners would read the Bible to her. Joan did not accept the Catholic doctrine on transubstantiation during the Eucharist – that the bread and the wine actually *become* the body and the blood of Jesus and she was resolute on the matter. The town bailiffs urged her to keep her strongly held views private but when challenged by clerics she was outspoken. The Bishop of Coventry and Lichfield asked Dr Anthony Draycot, the Diocesan Chancellor, to arraign Joan Waste on suspicion that she was a heretic. She was found guilty and beyond redemption. On 1st August 1556, Joan Waste was subjected to a lengthy sermon from Dr Draycot at All Saints Church and then led to Windmill Pit, Derby where she was burnt at the stake as a heretic. Windmill Pit was located to the west of the small turning circle seen today at the end of Lime Avenue off the Burton Road.

3.7 The Devonshire Chapel and burial vaults

As we noted earlier, there was a chapel dedicated to St Katharine located in the south-east corner of the mediaeval church. The altar in this chapel was removed during the Dissolution (1549 at All Saints) resulting in a diminished role for the chapel. However, towards the end of the 16th century, Elizabeth, Countess of Shrewsbury also known as Bess of Hardwick, purchased from the bailiffs and burgesses of Derby, the freehold of the South Quire as memorial ground for members of her family. Elizabeth had led a remarkable life. She was married [and widowed] four times and inherited great wealth from her deceased husbands. She used her wealth to build grand houses at Chatsworth and Hardwick and also founded a number of almshouses in Full Street behind All Saints Church.

Elizabeth commissioned Robert Smythson to supervise the excavation of a vault beneath St Katharine's Quire where she and her descendents would be buried. She also asked him to build a substantial monument in her memory (Fig. 3.8). This imposing edifice mainly composed of alabaster and black bituminous skeletal limestone from Derbyshire was constructed in St Katharine's Quire before Elizabeth died in 1608. A second large monument, dedicated to the memory of the second earl and countess was built in 1670. Both monuments were transferred to the Devonshire Chapel in the new church in 1725.

Over a period of just under 250 years there were 46 burials in the Cavendish vault including the first five Dukes of Devonshire and their Duchesses. In the first half of the 19th century, the original vault was almost full and so a second vault was excavated to the west of the first. However, only a few burials took place

before the Cavendish family decided in 1848 to open a new burial vault in Edensor. The vaults were sealed but access remained. In 1873 the monument to the second earl was dismantled and pews were installed, but the monument was restored in 1927. In 1973, the tombs in the vaults were found to be in a very poor state. They were restored to good order and the few tombs in the outer vault were transferred into spaces in the original vault. The outer vault was then converted into St Katharine's Chapel for quiet prayer with access from steps descending from the south aisle.

Figure 3.8: The monument dedicated to the memory of Elizabeth, Countess of Shrewsbury who died in 1608. The monument was built in the mediaeval church and transferred to the Devonshire Chapel [later Cavendish Chapel and now Cavendish Area] in the new church in 1725. From Cox & Hope (1881).

3.8 The Consistory Court

Historically, each diocese established a diocesan court or consistory where legal matters could be settled. In the 17th century, All Saints Church was in the Lichfield and

Coventry Diocese and the diocesan consistory court was located at Lichfield. However, All Saints Church possessed extra-episcopal powers of jurisdiction which permitted the church to grant marriage licences, probates of wills and letters of administration. In 1634, it was decided to build a Consistory Court comprising an official seat with desk and a table with other seats.

The Consistory was constructed out of oak and installed in the St Katharine's Quire in the south-east corner of the mediaeval church. This indicates that only part of the quire had been dedicated to the Cavendish family at this time. After the rebuilding of the church in 1725, the Consistory was positioned in the east end of the north aisle where it remains today. The oak structure was later complemented by the addition of a wrought iron candle sconce made by Robert Bakewell. The powers of ecclesiastic courts were rescinded in 1857.

3.9   The changes of font

Traditionally, fonts were intentionally large and made of stone so that they were fixed in position. Since the sacrament of baptism is a symbolic welcome of new members of the Christian community, the font was normally positioned at a convenient place close to the entrance to the church. From the accounts of the repairs to the font in the mediaeval church about 1620 to 1636, we learn that All Saints had a large sculptured stone font with a cover which was lifted by hemp ropes on pulleys. Many of the repairs related to the mechanism for lifting this cover.

This font survived the Dissolution but it was probably too 'superstitious' for the Puritans and it was removed from the church about 1647. The Puritans purchased a much simpler gilded alabaster basin. They also moved the place of baptism from near the church entrance to the chancel on the rational grounds that the congregation would be able see the newly baptised and their supporters.

In 1662, after the restoration, a new octagonal font with simple moulding (Fig. 3.9) was commissioned from Elias Grice for the price of £3 11s 8d [about £4,000 today] and located at the west end under the gallery. Thus we see that the font was returned to its traditional location close to the entrance of the church to symbolise the message of welcome. This font was replaced by a coloured marble font in Victorian times. In 1974, this marble font was replaced in turn by a new font made to an

elegant James Gibbs design. In addition, the Cathedral now has a portable font.

Figure 3.9: An engraving of the font made by Elias Grice in 1662 and placed at the west end of the mediaeval church. It was replaced by a marble font in Victorian times. From Cox & Hope (1881).

3.10   The hourglass on the pulpit

During the 17th century it was usual for the sermon to be over one hour in length. For the mutual benefit of the minister and the long-suffering congregation, an hourglass was attached to the side of the pulpit, fixed into an iron frame. The accounts show that in 1621, two shillings [about £120 today) was paid for a new frame and in 1643 Gilbert Ward was paid eight pence (about £40 today) to supply a new hourglass.

3.11   The churchyard runs out of space

During the 17th century, the mediaeval churchyard contained many graves and was planted with trees. It was traversed by a public path accessed by a gated turnstile at each end. By the 1630s the church yard was at full capacity and it was decided to raise the ground so that a new layer of graves could be made. The accounts show that huge amounts of gravel were brought in. The quantities were recorded as *loads* with each load perhaps equating to half a tonne and costing tuppence (2d) (about £10 today). In 1638 a delivery of 120 loads of gravel was followed by another delivery of 192 loads. In 1639, 50 loads were delivered; in 1657 there were 87 loads and in 1705 there were 180 loads. So well over 300 tonnes of gravel were delivered and the paths and gates were up-graded.

4: The building and architecture of the Cathedral Tower

4.1   The building of the Cathedral tower

The 16th century Cathedral tower that we see today replaced an earlier tower which was dismantled late in the reign of Henry VII. We know of the existence of this earlier tower because the Parish books record pointing of the 'old steeple' in 1475. The earlier tower is assumed to date from the 13th century or earlier because it is unlikely to have degraded to a ruinous state in just one hundred years if it had been built in the 14th century.

The building of the new tower was of course a major undertaking. All Saints was a Royal Free Chapel and a collegiate church of some standing and so it needed a fine tower of the highest quality which would reflect this importance. The tower was to be built in the contemporary late perpendicular style with decorative masonry and it was intended to compare favourably with any other tower in the country. The completed tower rose to 54 metres making it the second highest tower in England but the roof of the bell chamber is partially vaulted with stone work protruding to leave an octagonal opening in the centre with four squinches [small arches] in the corners. This robust structure may have been intended to carry a steeple or lantern.

The Church Wardens' minute books, which started in 1465, inform us that building of the tower had commenced by 1510 - the second year of the reign of Henry VIII. We also know that the tower was completed by 1532. So the construction took a minimum of 22 years. The Master Mason, at least in the latter years was John Otes who is reputed to have worked at King's College in Cambridge. The records show that in 1527 around Easter, John Otes was paid 3s 4d (about £600 today) for each full week and a bit less for shorter weeks.

4.2   Fund-raising: Robert Liversage the benefactor and the Church Ales events

As with most major projects, it was necessary instigate a major fund-raising campaign. A significant flow of funding came from Robert Liversage who was a generous benefactor. He gave regularly in the 1520s and the total amount given in 1527 was £5 13s 4d which was enough to pay John Otes' weekly wages for 34 weeks. Robert Liversage founded the Liversage Trust by his Will in 1529.

Church Ale events provided one of the principal sources of funding for Derbyshire churches.

Parishes such as Elvaston and Ockbrook would organise Church Ales events at least annually or when funds were needed for church repairs. Normally, two men would be chosen by the parish to act as wardens and masters of the feast. They would be responsible for collecting malt for brewing and corn for baking. They also asked householders to donate any items that might help with the entertainment. Then the ale would be brewed and cakes baked in readiness for the designated day. All the activities took place at a fair ground. The organised entertainment included mystery plays, Morris dancing, cudgel-playing, shooting at the butts and other sports. Money was raised from the sale of the ale and cakes and from the entry fees for the various activities. Further donations were levered from country gentlemen who came to watch the events.

In 1532, Thomas Parker and Thomas Hornby managed to raise an impressive £25 15s 6d (about £75,000 today) from a church ales event at Chaddesden, with an allowance of 34s 10d for expenses. Similarly at Brailsford, Thomas Turner raised £11 3s 4d with an allowance of 14s 5d for expenses. At Wirksworth the net sum of 28s 2d was raised.

There are two points for us to observe from this information. Firstly, the sums of money raised were quite substantial and would have made a welcome contribution to the cost of building the tower. Secondly, these examples demonstrate that fund-raising was taking place across Derbyshire and not just in All Saints parish. This reminds us that in the early 16th century, All Saints was a church of significant standing. It was a Royal Free Chapel and a collegiate church with a clerical team of canons and chaplains. The church itself was capacious and gloriously enriched with altars, shrines, pictures and statues. Thus, four centuries before it was hallowed as a Cathedral, All Saints Church was already regarded as the minster for the county of Derbyshire.

4.3   The decorative masonry of the tower

The tower was built from sawn blocks of Upper Carboniferous Sandstone from Derbyshire. It is built in the late perpendicular style and marks the end of the application of the gothic style in England until the gothic revival in the 19th century. The tower is 54 metres high, not including the pinnacles, and comprises three stages, each about the same in height. The tower is about 15 metres square at the base and becomes more slender in successive stages reducing to about 12 metres square at the top.

The first stage features the Tudor West Door with a niche on either side. The niches are each supported by a moulded corbel with a profusion of foliage and a face peering out known as *The Green Man* (Fig. 4.1).

Figure 4.1: A moulded corbel supporting the niche to the left of the West Door. The ornament consists of a thicket of foliage and rose blooms with a man's face peering out. *The Green Man*, as it is known, is thought to be a pagan allusion to fertility. PHB

The canopy of each niche is an elegant moulding with arches and pinnacles (Fig. 4.2). The two niches are empty. They have undoubtedly been restored (in 1845) and so we do not know if there were statues of saints in the niches before the Dissolution or before the Puritan attacks of 1643.

Figure 4.2: The beautiful ornamental canopy of the niche on the left side of the West Door. The canopy has three faces each comprising a central arch with trefoil moulding passing up into a decorative panel. The two pinnacles on either side of the central face culminate in a finial consisting of three small balls. PHB

Just above the architrave of the door there are some mouldings of a portcullis and of a Tudor rose. A band of heraldic shields is positioned above the architrave. The shields bear the Royal Coat of Arms of King Henry VIII featuring the lion *guardant* and the *fleur-de-lys* (Fig. 4.3).

Figure 4.3: A moulding of the Royal Coat of Arms of monarchs from Henry IV to James I. It is set in a quatrefoil frame and placed centrally in a band above the West Door. The quadrants of the shield feature the lion *guardant* and the *fleur-de-lys*. PHB

Above this band of shields we see the West Window decorated with perpendicular tracery (Fig. 4.4). We should note that when the tower was first built, the clock was positioned much lower than it is today. The exterior face was placed immediately below the West Window and there was a corresponding face in the nave.

Figure 4.4: The West Window shows decorative tracery in the late perpendicular gothic style. A hierarchical series of mullions subdivide the window into lights usually with trefoil heads. The window is composed of rectangular panes of clear glass. PHB

The south and north sides of the first stage are comparatively blank but at about 5 metres above the ground, there is a band with an inscription which reads:

𝔜oung men and maidens

This inscription is thought by tradition to refer to fund-raising efforts by the young people of Derbyshire. Some have suggested that the words may derive from Psalm 148 but Cox and

Hope (1881) contended that this did not make sense and the traditional explanation was more credible. The inscription on the south side has been restored while that on the north side, in a different orthography, may be original.

The tower is supported by two angle buttresses on each corner of the tower. These buttresses ascend in neatly overlapping stages to the top of the tower. Each stage culminates in a pinnacle surmounted by an elaborate moulded finial (Fig. 4.5). The next stage of the buttress commences from behind the pinnacle as the tower reduces incrementally in cross-sectional area.

Figure 4.5: The elegant buttress pinnacle at the top of the first stage on the south-west corner of the tower. The top of the buttress exhibits two gables each encrusted in ornamental moulding culminating in an apical *fleur-de-lys*. The buttress is surmounted by a pinnacle of tapered stonework supporting a highly ornate *fleur-de-lys* finial. PHB

The second stage of the tower features a large panel with decorative masonry on all four sides of the tower (Fig. 4.6). At the foot of the panel on the west and south sides we see the face of the Cathedral clock. The window behind the clock face brings light to the bell ringing loft.

The third [top] stage contains the bell chamber with its ring of ten bells. There is a single large louvre window on each side of the bell chamber

which direct the sound to the exterior. Each window is subdivided by three mullions and a single transom.

Figure 4.6: The large decorative panel on the west face of the second stage. The panel features three moulded pinnacles, each bearing three pairs of large crockets. Mullions subdivide the panel into blank lights with trefoil heads. PHB

The top of the tower is battlemented with decorative masonry forming the parapet (Fig.4.7).

Figure 4.7: A view of the battlemented top of the south face of the tower. Three gargoyles [G] project out from the base of the battlemented parapet. The corner pinnacles [P] rise from behind the tops of the angle buttresses [B]. PHB

20

Three gargoyles channel water away from the roof on each side of the tower. Each corner of the tower features a tall elegant pinnacle and there is an intermediate pinnacle on each side of the tower.

4.4 The repairs to the stonework

As one looks up at the splendid edifice which is the tower of the Cathedral Church of All Saints, it is easy to gain the impression that the fine tower has a strength and endurance which enables it to remain unchanged through time. In fact, the tower has been subject to the ravages of the weather for over 480 years and in that time it has needed much restoration and cleaning, sometimes quite extensively. Much of what we see has been restored and some more exposed parts have been restored many times.

The Church Warden accounts provide some insight into the types of repairs that have been required and the frequency of repairs. The lead roof has been repaired or renewed several times. In 1654, Bartholomew Shirly was paid £30 (about £6,000 today) for a new covering of lead on the roof. More repairs to the lead roof were needed in 1696; it cost 7s 9d just to haul the lead to the top of the tower. More repairs were needed in 1736 following a fire (Section 4.6). In 1830 the rooftop lead needed to be recast or renewed once again and this time the cost was £90 13s 0d (about £18,000 today).

The rooftop pinnacles have needed much attention. In 1629, the West Window and the pinnacles were repaired. Twenty-five years later, more work was needed on the West Window and the pinnacles at the cost of £5. On 28th August 1699, a committee was established to inspect and report on the pinnacles and the wind vanes attached to each one. The Committee concluded the vanes should be retained. In 1715, repair of the pinnacles cost £55. In 1806, repairs to the wind vanes cost £3 4s 0d. In 1823, new pinnacles cost £118 19 6d. Within five years, the pinnacles needed pointing and cramping with iron at a further cost of £41 19 8d. The intermediate rooftop pinnacles were restored in 1853 and the corner pinnacles were rebuilt in 1878, only 55 years after the last rebuild. The north-east pinnacle had to be replaced again in 1940 after an accident on 25th July when a rope mooring a barrage balloon became tangled around the pinnacle and the structure crashed to the ground.

By 1844, the tower was just over 300 years old and the extent of the decay was considerable.

The Parish decided that major exterior repairs would be necessary and so a fabric restoration committee was established. The Committee comprised 20 people and was chaired by the minister - The Revd Edward Lillingstone. It met on 13th May 1844 and Henry Isaac Stevens (1806-73) provided plans for consideration. The Committee decided to embark on fund-raising by subscription. On 20th May it was resolved to restore the tower to its original appearance, but there was some back-tracking later on this decision. On 19th July 1844, the Committee accepted the tender of £820 from Swinnerton and Lee for restoration of the tower using 100 metres of ashlar which is the name given to finely cut blocks of masonry.

On 16th September 1844 the Committee decided that the sundial in the south niche was neither useful nor ornamental and so it could be dispensed with. The following April it was agreed that the new stonework should be toned and coloured to correspond to the original very pale orange-pink sandstone. But following an intervention from Mr Stevens supported by a letter from Mr Bloxam a veteran ecclesiologist, the resolution to ensure a close match between the old and the new was abandoned. This decision is clearly evident as one examines the south-west buttresses of the first storey. The neat, clean bright new stone is very sharply delineated and can be traced up the edifice (Fig. 4.8).

Figure 4.8: Photograph of south angle buttress to show the clear junction between the finely sawn off-white sandstone [ashlar] used in the early Victorian restoration (1845) and the original sandstone, now weathered pale pink and pale brown-orange. PHB

In July 1845 the Committee accepted a further contract for £57 11s 10d for restoration of the West Door and the 189 steps of the tower. The subscription campaign managed to raise the splendid sum of £1,113 15s 0d (£200,000 today). So on 28th May 1846, the Committee was in the happy position of having a balance surplus of £6 10s 0d and decided to use this for further work on the West Door and have a celebratory dinner.

Further major repairs to the stonework were conducted in 1905 when scaffolding was erected over the entire tower and the body of the church. Much of the decorative panelling was restored at this time. During the 20th century, the Electricity Supply Station in Full Street enveloped neighbouring buildings in clouds of dust. Black grime progressively darkened the delicate colours and tones of the natural stone. When the 'evil' Electricity Supply Station was finally vanquished in the late 1960s, the Cathedral stonework was spruced up once again to coincide with the completion of the east end extension in 1972.

4.5 Spectacular 'flying' from the church tower

In 1732 the people were entertained by a Frenchman called Gillinoe who set up a rope stretching northwards from the parapet of the tower to St Michael's Church. He made a wooden board with a groove on the underside to act as a slot for the rope. He then mounted the board face down with the board supporting his abdomen. He then glided, arms and legs outstretched, at great speed down the rope firing a pistol and blowing a trumpet. Such was the speed of the descent that the friction of the rope passing through the groove generated much heat and a produced a trail of smoke. He must have made an impressive sight flying through the air trailing smoke like an 18th century equivalent of the Red Arrows. Of course his trail-smoke was limited to grey rather than red, white and blue. He performed his 'flying' act twice each day for three successive days and then went on to the next town. In 1734 another man successfully performed a similar flying act balancing a wheelbarrow containing a 13 year old boy.

On another occasion, an entertainer decided to attempt the extraordinary spectacle of sliding a donkey with lead weights on its legs, down a rope stretching from the top of the tower to the west end of St Mary Gate. The donkey was understandably unconvinced about the health and safety measures for this planned event and could be heard braying its concern from the top of the tower. It need not have worried. A large crowd gathered in St Mary Gate to witness the event. All was proceeding to plan until the weighted donkey was approaching the west end of St Mary Gate. At this point the rope broke and the donkey fell from the rope. Fortunately for the donkey its fall was cushioned by the crowd of onlookers and it was unhurt. Unfortunately for the crowd, it was a heavy donkey and there were some serious injuries. This accident put an end to any more 'flying' from the church tower.

4.6 Near disaster: the fire on the roof

In 1735 there was a near disaster for the church tower. The lead of the roof of the tower had developed two fractures which needed to be repaired. This required a hot iron to undertake soldering. Rather than carry the hot iron up the spiral staircase of the tower, the workmen elected to build a hearth of loose bricks on the tower roof. It appears that they must have left the heated bricks on the roof after completing the job because a few days later, smoke was spotted wafting from the tower roof. On investigation, it was discovered that the lead roof had melted and a supporting wooden beam had burnt to the point very close to failure. A disaster was only narrowly averted.

5: The re-building of the church: a tale of bitter conflict

5.1 The decay of the mediaeval church building

As we noted earlier (Section 3.1), the main body of the church was substantially rebuilt in the 14th century, so by the 17th century the structure was approaching 300 years old. The Dissolution of All Saints in 1549 resulted in the loss of the lands at Little Chester which had been a major source of income. Although six years later in 1555, Queen Mary had ensured that there would be sufficient resource to sustain two priests at All Saints for the future, the financial position was much weaker. Not only was the income from land and property reduced, but the removal of the altars, impoverishment of the decorations and overall loss of importance probably reduced the number of visitors to the church and the associated income.

Managing the upkeep of the physical estate and the church buildings in particular became a struggle. In 1629 Thomas Morton, Bishop of Coventry and Lichfield, criticised the Corporation of Derby which had held responsibility for the fabric since 1555, for the decayed state of the chancel. Repairs to the chancel were undertaken in 1637.

The situation was exacerbated during the Civil War and the Commonwealth Period when there was more destruction of Church treasures. Repairs to the South Porch are recorded for 1641 and in 1665 it was agreed to dismantle the two gable ends on the north side of the Church and to rebuild the pillars, the aisle windows and the roof. This major work was completed in 1676 at a cost of £26 (around £30,000 today). Despite this expenditure on repairs the decay continued, by the early 18th century the roof and the chancel were in a parlous state.

5.2 To repair or rebuild? That is the question

In 1713 the Parish Council recorded that the state of the main body of the Church was ruinous and it was doubtful if the building could be restored by repairs. Only very substantial building work would make a difference. On 9th July 1714 the Parish received a Brief - a Letter Patent from the Crown - which authorised a parish collection. A collection proceeded and raised £500 but a debate opened up regarding a key question. Should this fund be used for major restoration or should the body of the Church, extending eastwards from the tower, be completely dismantled to make way for a new building? This was the first mention of the possibility of a replacement building. Over the next nine years the debate developed into a bitter dispute with the most extraordinary climax.

For many people the disintegrating church building was a glorious fabric, much loved and revered for all its religious associations stretching over four centuries. Destruction of such a beautiful and ancient place of worship was unthinkable. For others the pragmatic solution was to sweep away the decaying building which was beyond repair and start again. However, this debate was not conducted with good grace and mutual understanding. The discussion became a heated dispute with much passion, jealousies, bad temper and disingenuous arguments.

The leading voice for rebuilding was the minister, The Revd Dr Michael Hutchinson, who was grandson of Bishop Hackett and was appointed by Derby Corporation as minister of All Saints Church in 1719. He was a man of great passion and energy but he came with a cauldron of attributes. The records suggest that he was inclined to be single-minded, confrontational, imperious, disingenuous and of short temper. Consequently, Dr Hutchinson tended to work solitarily rather than as a leader of a team but he was influential, persuasive and not without friends and supporters. His principal adversaries were the representatives of his employers - Derby Corporation - and he did not hesitate to use every possible tactic to win his position. As we shall see, he was also prepared to revoke his own decisions and change his personal position when it suited him to do so.

On 16th November 1719, Dr Hutchinson and ten others met in the vestry and agreed to ask Mr Smith of Warwick to send a list of works and a quotation for the building of a new Church that the Trustees should think fit-for-purpose and pleasing to the parishioners. It was agreed to acquaint the Mayor of the Corporation with the proposal so that he may also agree. By early 1722, there was a formal proposition to demolish the old church and erect a new one. Funding for this rebuild would be by subscription. But by August 1722, there were various objections to the architectural plans and the contractor. So the church wardens were asked to procure a model of the proposed building for the cost of no more than

10 guineas (£10.50). However, the model did not assuage objections from a large number of parishioners and the Derby Corporation to the proposed destruction of the mediaeval church. Conservative parishioners eventually agreed to the establishment of a Committee comprising the minister, the church wardens, William Woolley (Mayor) and others making a total membership of 14 and requiring a quorum of nine. As the Committee meetings proceeded, it became clear that the Committee was equally divided regarding whether or not the old church should be destroyed. The Corporation disliked the proposed rebuilding scheme.

Dr Hutchinson had given a pledge at the time of his appointment that he would observe the extra-episcopal character of All Saints Church. Accordingly, he did not seek confirmation of his appointment by the diocesan bishop. However, Dr Hutchinson went further than this to demonstrate the independence of All Saints Church. When the bishop made a visitation to All Saints, Dr Hutchinson publicly protested about his right to make the Visit. He supported the Corporation in refusing the bishop a seat in the Chancel and obliged the bishop to sit in the Consistory Court in the north aisle. In the Cathedral Church of today, with the Bishop's Throne placed in the chancel, it is almost unbelievable that the church of 1720 could have been so hostile to a visit from the bishop.

Dr Hutchinson chaired the Committee and progressively wore down his opponents on the Committee by attrition. Some of these members ceased to attend. He bolstered his case for rebuilding by voluntarily holding himself personally responsible for the great expense to be incurred. However, he did add the caveat that his wife was not included in this financial assurance because she could not tolerate trouble. A resolution was finalised at a sparsely attended meeting in the vestry in mid-February 1723. A plan drawn-up by James Gibbs (Fig.5.1), the architect who had designed St Martin-in-the-Fields in London, was set before the Committee and accepted.

It was decided to ask Mr Smith, a builder, to provide an estimate of the costs of the materials and labour as soon as possible so that the Trustees appointed by the Parish could inspect the plan to rebuild the church. There was no mention of the Trustees needing to *approve* the plan. The Corporation received the architectural plan but thought that there was more time available for consideration and a final decision would be taken when Mr Smith had submitted his quotation for the cost.

Figure 5.1: An engraving of James Gibbs the architect of the rebuilt church (1725). DC (1972)

5.3 Hutchinson's pre-emptive decision

Let us take stock of the formal position. By mid-February 1723, Dr Hutchinson had obtained the agreement of the Committee to the architectural plan prepared by James Gibbs. But he had not yet convinced his patrons or many influential townsmen of the merits of rebuilding, He did not yet have a quotation for cost of building the new church and most importantly, he had not secured the *approval* of his employers Derby Corporation for the overall plan or the cost of rebuilding. Nevertheless, on the morning of 18th February 1723 before day-break, he admitted a large body of workmen to the church and they proceeded to dismantle the interior fittings, the roofs and they started to raze the fabric. In a few hours they destroyed the once splendid mediaeval church.

5.4 Fund-raising for the new church

Dr Hutchinson had undoubtedly taken a pre-emptive decision which would not please his employers (Derby Corporation) or many of his parishioners. So he embarked upon a charm offensive. He explained how sorry he was about pressing ahead but he promised to take full responsibility upon himself to raise the funds needed for the rebuild by subscription. He would lead the fund raising process and he would contribute £40 of his own money to the fund. Derby Corporation felt that it had little option other than to accept the *fait accomplis* and furthermore it made a £200 contribution to the subscription fund. Dr Hutchinson toured the country, visiting distinguished people in London, Oxford and Cambridge. Amongst many others, he succeeded in obtaining contributions from Sir Robert Walpole and Sir Isaac Newton and managed to raise a subscription fund of £3,000.

Building was already underway even though the money required was not yet in place. The cost of the rebuild was now estimated to be about £3,500 (about £3-4 million today) and so, although the subscription fund was substantial, it was still about £500 short of the total needed. It would therefore be necessary to devise a way of raising more money.

5.5 Controversial fund-raising: selling seats

Dr Hutchinson now embarked on a new fund-raising scheme which was destined to bring more heartache and strife to the parish. Hitherto, parishioners attending church could sit wherever they pleased. However, Dr Hutchinson believed that selling the right to occupy seats could raise significant and precious additional income. He proposed to sell the rights to 40 seats in the new church. Persons of appropriate societal rank or position would be approached to ask if they would like to purchase, for a sum to be negotiated, the right for the purchaser or a member of their family to occupy specified seats at church services. Dr Hutchinson proposed to conduct this process himself. *He* would decide *which people* would be approached, *which seats* they would be offered and the payments that they would make.

This was not the first time that seats had been appropriated. In 1704 the parish council had accepted an offer of £20 (about £20,000 today) from John Osborne for the *right* for his family to occupy three seats close to the bishop's seat in the south aisle. It was a decision that the Council had regretted because there were so many problems. Mr Osborne objected to lesser persons such as servants sitting close-by and he refused to pay for repairs because he did not *own* the seats. Trouble rumbled on for 15 years and so other similar offers were declined.

Unsurprisingly, there were strong objections to Dr Hutchinson's plan. Parishioners observed that 40 seats represented a considerable proportion of the seating area which would become unavailable to those not favoured by the invitation to buy. Even those who had been invited to buy seats, were upset that they had not been offered the seats which their rank or position warranted. The entire plan was considered by many as totally contrary to church tradition and unacceptable. But Dr Hutchinson disregarded all of these views.

A petition was submitted to the Corporation of Derby Common Council. Signed by no less than the church wardens and 70 parishioners, the petition stated that 70% of the Parish contended that they should not be deprived of the rights which they and their ancestors had always enjoyed. Dr Hutchinson countered by asking the bishop (the same one whom he had refused a seat in the chancel) to arrange for a Commission to confirm his disposal of seats. Dr Hutchinson hoped that the bishop would consider the matter during the service of his congregation at St Michael. But the bishop refused. Dr Hutchinson requested this intervention despite the expectation of Derby Corporation that episcopal influence should be minimal. George Statham, one of the church wardens, announced that a parish meeting would take place in the Church, but Dr Hutchinson retaliated, threatening to indict him for brawling in the Church and he declared that the proposed meeting would be illegal. So on 27th September 1725, a parish meeting was held in the Town Hall. An order was drawn-up and signed by William Fitzherbert, Samuel Cooper (the Mayor) and 43 parishioners. The order stated that seats in the rebuilt Church are not to be sold or disposed of without the consent of the church wardens and the majority of parishioners. Furthermore, the church wardens were indemnified against cost and charges regarding giving notice of the meeting at St Michael's Church.

The diocesan bishop was also strongly opposed to the scheme to sell the rights to seats in the rebuilt church. A Commission was set-up and attended to hear evidence. However Dr Hutchinson asked for the work of the Commission to be adjourned and in the interests of peace, this was agreed by opponents of the scheme. Dr Hutchinson now went into apologetic mode. On 15th October 1725, Dr Hutchinson sent a letter of apology to the Mayor. Derby Corporation reciprocated by passing an order in Common Council appreciating the letter. On 21st October 1725, a parish meeting also agreed a conciliatory response to the letter. As in the old church, a few seats would be reserved for the minister, Derby Corporation and members of the merchant chambers. But the parish resolved not to sell seats in the rebuilt church; seats would be used as they were before. The shortfall in income raised by subscription would be raised by other means.

On 1st November 1725 the parish agreed a partial reversal of the resolution accepted just 11 days before - which must have given Dr Hutchinson some satisfaction. In a compromise solution, it was decided to sell by auction, *six double seats* instead of the originally proposed 40 single seats. The purchased seats could be used by the purchasers, their heirs and by those to whom they assigned the seats. The sums paid for the paired seats ranged from £35 14s 0d paid by Mr Parr to £90 6s 0d paid by Mr Franceys. The sale realised a healthy £475 13s 0d and, together with six guineas raised for burials in vaults, was sufficient to make good the deficit in the subscription fund.

5.6 The new church opens but with more upset

Fund-raising and rebuilding progressed simultaneously and by November 1725, the new church was ready. The inaugural sermon was preached on 21st November 1725 in an atmosphere of harmony and Dr Hutchinson was complimented on the conclusion of the work. Indeed it was a remarkable achievement to have raised the funds and overseen the entire rebuilding of the main body of the church in just 33 months.

But all was not well for long. In December 1725 a new dispute ensued. On 14th December 1725, the parish books record an order indicating that the church wardens *and* the minister may guide the members of the congregation to the seats as they think fit. But the church wardens complained that Dr Hutchinson was not consulting them. On one highly embarrassing occasion, two ladies sat together in a non-assigned pew and Dr Hutchinson, in full view of the congregation, ordered the two ladies to move to another pew. The next Sunday he placed Mr Yates in the vacated seats. This action was clearly highly embarrassing to the ladies concerned and the church wardens felt that their responsibilities had been transgressed. So they took action. On 27th December 1725, the order of 14th December was revoked. A new order was approved restricting the authority for the allocation of seats in the church to the church wardens and parishioners with no mention of the minister.

5.7 The resignation farrago

Early in 1726 Dr Hutchinson was clearly unhappy. He approached Alderman Samuel Cooper, the Mayor, at a meeting and gave notice of his resignation which would take effect at Michaelmas 1726 (29th September). The Mayor did not accept the resignation and asked to meet Dr Hutchinson at The Vine to discuss and resolve the differences. They agreed to meet on Friday 25th February 1726 but on the preceding Wednesday, Dr Hutchinson wrote to the Mayor saying that he would not be meeting on Friday because he had already decided to leave at Michaelmas: thereafter, the Corporation would have to manage the affairs of the church. He added, "I pray God to forgive all those who without any cause have been my enemys." [sic] He signed off "I am Sir your humble servant, Michael Hutchinson."

The Mayor and colleagues from the Corporation did go to The Vine and sent Dr Hutchinson a further invitation to meet them there - but the minister refused. They decided to call a Common Hall of the Corporation and inform them of the planned resignation. The Common Hall accepted the minister's resignation. Soon after, they sent a communication to The Revd William Chambers, who had at least one relative on the Corporation, indicating that he would be nominated for the position of Minister of the Church of All Saints Derby, if he was interested. Mr Chambers travelled from London to Derby and met with Dr Hutchinson who was complimentary about him.

In a communication, Dr Hutchinson confirmed his resignation and said that he was content for Mr Chambers to be his successor. Indeed, he would prefer Mr Chambers to anyone else. At the end of May 1726, Mr Chambers announced his intention to accept the nomination. But almost immediately, in a short letter sent to the Mayor, Dr Hutchinson retracted his resignation. In his letter, Dr Hutchinson said that he did not know if he had given any legal notice of his intention to resign as minister of All Saints. He now intended to continue to at least Lady Day in March 1727. Since this would enable Dr Hutchinson to oversee all the final work at the Church, the Corporation consented to absolve Dr Hutchinson from his promise to resign at Michaelmas 1726 on condition that he sign a legal document pledging to withdraw on Lady Day 1727. This was drawn up and signed by Dr Hutchinson on 3rd August 1726. He agreed to *absolutely* resign on 25th March 1727. But as this new date approached, the minister reported that he had discovered arrears of small tithes due to him. These arrears amounted to the significant sum of £40 - the exact amount of Dr Hutchinson's own contribution to the subscription fund. The

Corporation helpfully promised to refund any arrears that Dr Hutchinson could evidence.

The Corporation also resolved that a present should be given to Mrs Hutchinson in the form of 20 broad pieces [one broad is 23 shillings] [total £23] to be paid ten days after the resignation has taken effect. Dr Hutchinson was also offered a solicitor to recover the tithes but he declined this assistance because this mechanism would not meet his costs. Dr Hutchinson wanted more money and now refused to leave unless £30 was given to him in cash, in addition to the present to his wife. The Corporation in turn refused to give him the £30 he demanded and so Dr Hutchinson revoked his decision to resign and declared that he was *not* going to leave.

On the Sunday after Lady Day 1727, the Mayor, Town Clerk and Mr Chambers demanded that Dr Hutchinson step down as minister in accordance with the instrument dated 3rd August 1726 but he refused. At the service on 16th April 1727, Dr Hutchinson was permitted to officiate but Council advised the Corporation to introduce The Revd William Chambers the nominated new minister to the congregation at All Saints. As it turned out, Dr Hutchinson had a commitment in Lichfield but he asked his friend and kindred soul The Revd Henry Cantrell (1685-1773) of St Alkmund's Church to occupy the pulpit. Apparently, Mr Cantrell rivalled Dr Hutchinson in his love of confrontation and litigation. Thus on 16th April 1727 the problem developed into a full crisis at All Saints Church.

Mr Cantrell went to All Saints Church for the morning service at 10.00 am and put on his surplice and occupied the minister's seat. But the sexton declined to ring the bells. The Mayor and his Committee kept the congregation waiting while they debated in a neighbouring inn the action that they would take at the service. At 10.45 am the service bell rang and Mr John Bagnold, the Mayor in his gown, preceded by the mace bearer, two sergeants and four aldermen in their gowns of office followed by Mr Chambers proceeded up the main aisle. Mr Cantrell was in the minister's seat. The aldermen took their allocated pews but the Mayor proceeded to the minister's seat and leaning over, he addressed Mr Cantrell. Mr Bagnold's friends claim that in a low quiet voice he remonstrated with Mr Cantrell on his presence there when Derby Corporation had appointed Mr Chambers as the new minister. He reminded Mr Cantrell that he should be ministering to his own parishioners. Dr Hutchinson's associates complained that the Mayor grievously insulted Mr Cantrell and shook his staff of authority in a threatening manner. The Mayor, they claimed, generated 'prodigious noise and clammer - much to the consternation, terror and disturbance of the congregation'. When the litany was ended, Mr Chambers went up before the usual time to the pulpit to present a sermon. At this moment, Mr Cantrell rose in his seat and in the name of the bishop and Dr Hutchinson, prohibited Mr Chambers from preaching. But the new minister persisted and gave a most appropriate sermon on the subject of living peaceably with all men. The Mayor sent a special messenger to the bishop who was in London, to enquire if he had authorised the protest from Mr Cantrell. The bishop replied in a letter received on Saturday 22nd April 1727 that he had given no such authority.

On Sunday 23rd April 1727, one week after the first confrontation, the Mayor went again to All Saints Church with Mr Chambers and once again found Mr Cantrell there. The Mayor accused Mr Cantrell of wrongfully claiming the authority of the bishop on 16th April in front of the congregation. During the service, Mr Cantrell passed Mr Chambers who was turned towards the altar and went up into the pulpit where for the second time, claiming the authority of the bishop and Dr Hutchinson, he prohibited the ministry of 'intruders'.

It was agreed to resolve the matter by going to arbitration conducted by Mr Vice-Chamberlain Stanhope and Mr Turner. A bond for £500 was arranged by which each side pledged to abide by the arbitrator's decision. As a preliminary, Dr Hutchinson pledged, in writing and in spoken word, to resign the pulpit on the following Sunday. On 15th August 1727, Dr Hutchinson sent a letter to the Mayor indicating that he would give up the pulpit the following Sunday *providing that* there were no proceedings against Mr Cantrell. The Mayor gave the assurance immediately but Dr Hutchinson found more excuses and stayed on.

On 22nd September 1727, Dr Hutchinson instigated proceedings against Mr Bagnold, the Mayor, who was required to answer charges regarding his behaviour in All Saints Church in April 1727 to be heard at the Consistory Court in Lichfield. At the request of the Mayor, the court granted a dispensation that the Commission of the Court was permitted to sit at Derby. The Commission sat at All Saints Church on 13th February 1728. There were strong differences in the evidence. Dr Hutchinson's supporters claimed that the Mayor uttered 'an insolent, foul-mouthed braggadocio which terrified the congregation by its outrageous violence of language and gestures'. Other witnesses stated that the Mayor made necessary and quiet protest against the illegal actions of Dr Hutchinson's substitute. The Mayor's voice, they believed, was barely audible five metres away. The Commission declined to take into consideration the pledge from Dr Hutchinson to vacate the pulpit. The focus of the Commission's proceedings was on whether or not the Mayor brawled, as alleged, in church.

On 14th May 1728, the Consistory Court pronounced against the Mayor and fined him £37, a very significant sum [£30,000 today], including costs. Furthermore it was stated in a document that the Mayor was to be excommunicated or debarred the privilege of hearing divine service and must not enter any church or chapel for a period of time to be determined by the bishop or appointee. It is not known whether this sentence was pronounced or enforced. Dr Hutchinson now accused Derby Corporation of the mismanagement of charities. The Corporation retaliated by insisting that Dr Hutchinson should place the financial accounts relating to the rebuilding before the Commission. But the Parish declared the order illegal and inconvenient. Dr Hutchinson no longer attended the meetings of the Parish Council.

Dr Hutchinson finally left All Saints Church at Michaelmas - 29th September 1728. This was more than two and a half years after his first letter of resignation and two years after his first resignation date. He moved to a new position at Packington in north Leicestershire but died there on 10th January 1730.

Four pamphlets, published in 1728, give contrasting accounts of the altercation between Mr Cantrell and the Mayor of Derby at All Saints Church on 16th and 23rd April 1727. Three of these pamphlets were written by Dr Hutchinson and his friends: the fourth presents the other side of the story recorded by the Mayor of Derby Corporation.

(i) The first, prepared by Dr Hutchinson, is titled an impartial account of a great disturbance on 16th and 23rd April (1728) occasioned by the mayor brawling, boisterous and using scurrilous language in a Holy Place. There was also usurpation of the pulpit by Mr Chambers in the morning and by Mr Winter in the afternoon. The pamphlet describes the prosecution of the mayor in the Consistory Court of Lichfield. (1728)

(ii) A review of the proceedings written by Thomas Houghton, the Mayor in 1727. (1728)

(iii) A reply to the review - printed and sold by Sam Hodgkinson in Sadlergate. (1728)

(iv) Dr Hutchinson vindicated. Printed and sold by Sam Hodgkinson, Sadler Gate. (1728)

5.8 The final rebuilding accounts

The Parish and the Commissioners refused to approve Dr Hutchinson's financial accounts of the rebuilding. Dr Hutchinson had not fulfilled his promise of taking on the responsibility for the full funding of the new building himself and many invoices had been left unpaid. It therefore became necessary to raise more money. Various properties were sold and Mrs Hutchinson sent £155. The outstanding subscriptions monies amounted to £137 16s 6d but the church wardens only managed to recover a small fraction of this - £11 0s 6d.

James Gibbs the architect was paid just £25 for the architectural plans and Robert Bakewell was paid a total of £338 10s 0d (£300,000 today) for the beautiful ironwork chancel screen and the Cathedral gates (removed in 1873). Some payments were made as much as five years after the completion of the rebuilding. The Church Warden's accounts for 1730/31 show that final invoices were paid in favour of Mr Smith, the main builder (£105), Mr Hall for the Marble Altar (£126), Mr Manning, Clerk of Works and Joiner (£58), Mr Bakewell for the ironwork, (£157), Mr Redfern (£4 15s 0d) and Mr Trimmer (£100) coming to a total of about £550. The final total cost of rebuilding the church was £4,037 3s 8d (about £4 million today). After all the invoices had been settled, there was a residual balance of £13 15s 10d.

5.9 The building of a Parish Workhouse

In 1728 shortly before the departure of Dr Hutchinson, a decision was taken to build a parish workhouse. There were of course no funds available for this cause because the accounts for the rebuilding project were not yet finally settled. The construction of a Workhouse in Walker Lane was considered a priority and so the decision was taken on 22nd July 1728 to sell twelve properties. These properties had been bringing in an annual rent of £13 13s 3d, but despite the loss of future income, it was decided that they should be sold. The sale realised £256. Nine months later on 29th April 1729, the parish accepted an estimate of £330 for the building works from Mr Trimmer, a local builder contractor who had helped build the new Church. The Parish Workhouse functioned until the building and land were sold by the authority of the Poor Law Commissioners on 20th September 1841.

5.10 Selling Church property to raise funds

During mediaeval times All Saints Church acquired many acres of pasture and arable land as well as residential properties and at least one public house. This estate amounted to a significant commercial operation which generated important rental income. The holdings were located in north and south Derby and came through grants, purchases and bequests. However, when the Church embarked upon major projects, particularly in the period 1723 to 1735, much property was sold to fund the projects. These disposals resulted in an immediate reduction in rental income and constituted a permanent loss of income generating resource. The selling of property to fund the building of a Parish Workhouse was just one example. There were several more.

There is a recorded sale in 1513 of a house and a garden in Bag Lane (now East Street) for 12/- (60p) to be paid over two years. This sale may have helped fund the building of the tower. But most disposals are recorded in the period 1726 to 1735. The sale of a house in St Peter's Parish in 1726 was followed in 1728 by the fund-raising for the Parish Workhouse.

In 1731 there was still a deficit in the accounts for the rebuilding of the church completed six years earlier in 1725 and so more fund-raising was deemed necessary. Much land was effectively sold. This included six acres of pasture and 2½ acres of arable land in Normanton; one acre on the Old Meadows in Derby and one acre at Chequer Close. This land was passed to Matthew Howe who paid £240 for a one thousand year lease at a peppercorn rent.

One year later in 1732, there was a new project in the recently completed body of the Church. Money was needed to build a gallery to house an organ at the west end of the nave. All Saints owned a lucrative hostelry known as the Angel Inn in the bustling Cornmarket. (The Angel Inn formerly stood towards the southern end of the site currently occupied by Primark. It was demolished in 1969). This public house had a long history of providing a good rental income. In 1657 Thomas Bourne had taken out a 60 years tenancy for the annual rent of £10. In 1686 another lease was agreed at the same rent. However, on 17th April 1732, it was decided to sell the Angel Inn to raise funds to build the gallery at All Saints. The sale raised the substantial sum of £210 but this was insufficient. A year later, two houses in St Mary's Gate were sold to Mr Hugh Bateman raising a further £30 towards the gallery project.

In the 19th century the cash proceeds of a major opportunistic sale were re-invested. In 1837 the parish sold lands in the Old Meadows to North Midland Railway for £709. This time the money was invested.

6: The architecture of the new church and the 19th century re-ordering

6.1   The architecture of the new church

Since the destructive event of 1723, there have been many who have lamented the loss of the mediaeval fabric of the old church. There can be no doubt that the former 14th century gothic body of the church and the early 16th century late perpendicular style tower must have appeared as a glorious building of splendour and beauty. Nevertheless, the new body of the church, completed in the Roman Baroque style in 1725, quite quickly generated a sense of pride and it formed the centre piece of the fine engraving of the east prospect of Derby (Fig. 6.1) published by Samuel and Nathaniel Buck just three years later in 1728.

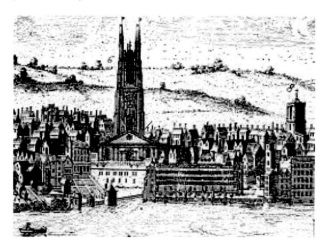

Figure 6.1: Part of an engraving of the east prospect of Derby published by Samuel and Nathaniel Buck in 1728. Note the pediment above the east wall of the new church building, now largely hidden by the extension completed in 1972. © November 2014 Derby Museums Trust.

By 1722, Dr Michael Hutchinson minister at All Saints, had already commissioned Church architect James Gibbs to draw up a plan for a new church before any formal decision had been taken to replace the existing building. There were no funds in advance for re-building and so the new church building needed to be designed with affordability in mind.

In his long life, James Gibbs (1662-1754) (Fig. 5.1) came to his architectural career quite late. He went out to Rome in 1704 at the age of 42 to train for the Catholic priesthood but he was inspired to take up architecture and with his deep knowledge of Roman architecture, he became a leading exponent of the Roman Baroque style in the early decades of the 18th century. In 1720, he prepared the design for St Martin-in-the-Fields at Trafalgar Square. For the London church, Gibbs planned a large portico frontage with a pediment supported by Roman Doric columns.

But All Saints Church already had a very fine gothic tower which provided a west entrance and so the challenge for James Gibbs was to design a building for the body of the church that would complement the extant tower. Gibbs adapted the Roman Baroque design that he had prepared for the church of St Martin-in-the-Fields in London. The outline of the exterior is a simple rectangular form. At the west end there are entrance doors leading directly into the north and south aisles (Fig. 6.2). The doors display the Gibbs' *surround* design in which the architrave features a large central keystone with *voussoirs* on either side. Large sculptured stones are intercalated into the architrave on either side of the door. Each aisle door is surmounted by a triangular pediment. Above each pediment there is a large round window with plain glass and framed by a Gibbs' *surround*. On the north and south sides of the building, a series of tall windows again show the typical Gibbs' *surround* architrave. The parapet walls on the north and south sides of the church display fine balustrades.

Figure 6.2: View of the Roman Baroque exterior of the Cathedral Church designed by James Gibbs. This view from the south-west shows the south aisle door, the round window above and the tall windows of the south aisle all exhibiting Gibbs' *surround* stonework. Note the balustrades which make up the parapet. This is an enlarged part of a drawing by J Bailey circa 1880. From Cox & Hope (1881).

The interior of the Church was beautifully designed to give a sense of space and light. The main body of the Church completed in

1725, comprises a barrel vaulted nave, a north aisle, south aisle, chancel, sanctuary and Devonshire Chapel. The roof of the nave is supported by a series of five pairs of Doric columns. Each column has a dosseret placed above the capital (Fig. 6.3).

Figure 6.3: An engraving of the interior of All Saints showing the Gibbs' design and the 1725 box pews. Note the Doric columns capped with dosserets [arrows]. In this picture by N Rowbottom in 1849 we see additional seating in the main aisle. The picture pre-dates the Prince Albert Memorial windows installed in 1863. From *Life in Bygone Derbyshire* (1977).

The dosserets raise the spring points for the arches of the groin-vaults which make up the ceiling of the north and south aisles. To maximise the feeling of simplicity and brightness, the original windows were fitted with plain glass allowing light to stream unfiltered into the building. This is very evident in the engraving. In 1725, and in keeping with James Gibbs' precepts, there was no gallery. An observer in the sanctuary could see the West Window in the church tower.

However, within one year, there was a lobby pressing for the construction of a gallery to house an organ and Gibbs' precept of vision and light was already under threat. By 1743, a gallery was built and an organ installed (Section 6.3).

On completion in 1725 the church was fitted out with high-sided box pews with seats on three sides and a door on the fourth side. This type of pew was very common in the early 18th century. Box pews had one particular benefit. They protected the congregation from cold draughts which inhabited unheated churches. There was indeed no heating in the new church of All Saints in 1725.

The high sides also tended to discourage members of the congregation from peering around at other people in the church rather than concentrate on the solemnity of the occasion. Of course, the high sides also made it difficult to see the altar, especially for those who happened to be seated in the box pews with their backs to the altar.

6.2 The Chancel Screen by Robert Bakewell

The nave was separated from the chancel by an exceedingly fine wrought ironwork screen crafted by the local blacksmith Robert Bakewell (Fig 6.4). The combination of beautiful filigree ironwork and the lightness of the structure enabled the chancel and nave to be demarcated without any sense of occlusion. The chancel screen originally crossed the church at the position of the second pair of columns from the east wall, where we see it today. However, as we will see, the chancel screen was destined to be repeatedly altered and shifted to please the idiosyncrasies of the moment.

Like James Gibbs who prepared the architectural plans, Robert Bakewell (1682-1752) was asked to start work on the ironwork screen to separate the nave and chancel in 1722, *before* the decision had been taken to demolish the mediaeval church. The work of art produced by Bakewell is so remarkable we should know about his background.

Robert Bakewell was the son of Sampson and Mary Bakewell who lived in Uttoxeter. There was already a family connection with blacksmithing. Sampson was a blacksmith and Mary was a daughter of a blacksmith. It was also an educated family. In 1694, when Robert was 12, his father died leaving a cabinet of violas, two harpsichords and many books. His mother Mary remarried in 1696 and Robert, now 14, was apprenticed to a blacksmith in London. There he made railings for a house owned by Thomas Coke who lived in St James Place. During the 1690s Bakewell was influenced by Jean Tijou who was an expert in the art of repoussé in which three-dimensional ironwork is beaten out of the sheet of metal from the back and then sharpened by

The Church - 1725

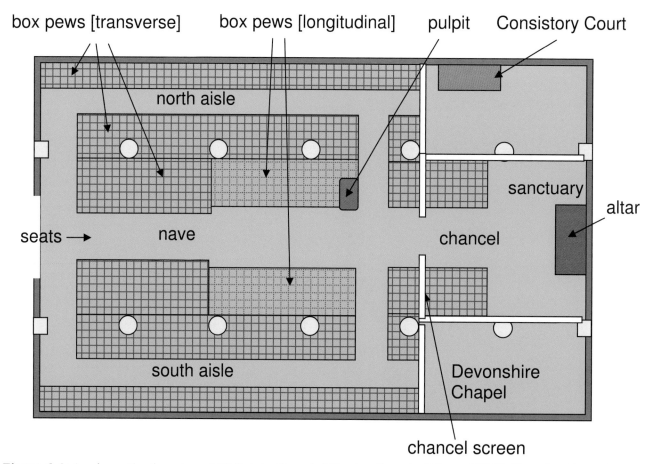

box pews [transverse]   **box pews [longitudinal]**   **pulpit**   **Consistory Court**

north aisle

seats →   nave   chancel   sanctuary   altar

south aisle   Devonshire Chapel

chancel screen

Figure 6.4: A schematic plan view of All Saints Church following the rebuilding of 1725. Note the Chancel Screen and the additional sections of grille separating off the Devonshire Chapel and the Consistory Court. PHB

chasing from the front. Jean Tijou did work at St Paul's Cathedral and on a balcony at Chatsworth. Robert Bakewell was not an expert in repoussé, but he did use the process to produce beautiful swirling *Acanthus* leaves, hart's tongue and water leaves.

The chancel screen, completed in 1725, is one of Bakewell's masterpieces. It was severely mauled in Victorian times and only the central section survived the 19th century, re-positioned in front of the sanctuary. In 1905 Edwin Haslam installed elegant new grilles around the Devonshire Chapel and the Consistory Court (Figure 6.5). Robert Bakewell's central section with gate, pilasters and overthrow was restored to its original position in 1927.

Bakewell also made some of the church fittings including the ironwork frame for the marble-top altar; the corporation pew with sword rest; the mace stand and lady mace holder; the communion rails which were a variation of the baluster design with lyre form, scrolls, water leaves and gilded flame tufts; and the candle sconce which is fixed to the Consistory Court.

The Consistory Court was first installed in 1634 and moved to its present position in 1725 on completion of the new church.

Figure 6.5: Gilded *Acanthus* leaves on the wrought iron screen made by Edwin Haslam in 1905 to replace the lost section of grille made by Robert Bakewell in 1725. These leaves are located to the right of the entrance to the Cavendish Area. PHB

6.3   The earlier organs at All Saints Church

All Saints Church is thought to have had two organs during the 15th and 16th centuries. The inventories for 1569/70 and 1594/5 refer to the lead weights which were used to compress the bellows. One organ was probably located in the rood loft. They probably wore out and did not survive the 16th century. An organ would not have found favour with the Puritans and so All Saints was without an organ until the 18th century.

In 1726, just one year after completion of the new church, there was a lobby to build a gallery and install an organ. But with the accounts not settled, this matter was put into abeyance for five years. In 1731, it was decided that the first step was to create a gallery at the west end which could accommodate an organ and some choristers. We recall (Section 5.9) that the Angel Inn in Cornmarket was sold to help raise the money needed. A central gallery was built in 1731/2 and an organ committee was established in 1733. Eventually an organ was installed ten years later in 1743.

The organ appears to have been second hand. Bernard Smith made the instrument in 1703. It was large and housed in a classical 18th century case comprising four-towers 7 m high and 4 m deep (Fig. 6.6).

Figure 6.6: The original organ case (1703) which enclosed the organs at All Saints between 1743 and 1939. The case has four-towers with a classical cornice. Only one small brace of cherubs [arrow] has survived and is now attached to the choir organ (Fig, 7.7). From Tomkins & Mallender 1973.

The church was delighted to possess an organ once again and appointed William Denby as organist. An organ recital was planned in 1745, but this was cancelled because the organ, now over 40 years old, was proving unreliable. In 1747 The Hon. John Stanhope donated £50 for repairs to the organ and it continued in service.

By 1807 the organ had celebrated its hundredth birthday and was considered worn out and beyond repair. Within a year, an organ committee had raised £600 by subscription and taken a firm decision to commission Thomas Eliot to make and install a new organ. The estimated cost of the instrument was £800. Eliot recommended including a Coupler Stop to make the Great Organ play *with* the Choir Organ and thirteen additional pedal pipes. He believed that with these features, this instrument would surpass any previous organ built in England. He rashly agreed to pay £100 for the old great organ but later regretted this offer when he discovered its poor state. All Saints therefore agreed to give him the choir organ as well. The latter may be the organ that Eliot set up in the Gedling Parish Church in Nottingham in 1808.

The new instrument at All Saints had 867 pipes in the Great Organ, 348 pipes in the choir organ and 252 pipes in the swell organ making a total of 1,467 pipes. Installation into the 1703 organ casing was completed on 25th September 1808. The new organ was heavier than its predecessor and so two metal columns were inserted under the gallery to provide additional support. These columns were clad in oak and then carved in the Roman Ionic style to resemble the existing columns. The final cost was £1,000 [about £250,000 today]. There was of course no electricity and so the wind was provided by hand bellows. One large pair of horizontal bellows had five feeds and another pair of bellows had two feeds.

In 1831 a performance of the *Messiah* was planned by A Buckingham and advice was sought from W Woodward of St Mary's RC Church regarding the quality and condition of the instrument. He declared it to be one of the most beautiful instruments that he had ever heard; the tone and quality were considered extremely good. He identified one technical fault which could be corrected by a specialist. In 1841, one hundred years after the building of the central gallery, new side galleries were added on the north and south to accommodate more choristers and congregation.

During the 19th century it was the fashion to make organs more romantic and so in 1879, the time came for Eliot's organ to be replaced. The organ chosen was a Stringer organ with a three-manual console, 38 speaking stops and 2,080 pipes. Some of Eliot's pipes were retained and the 1703 casing was also retained. This kept the cost down to £500 – about half the cost of the Eliot organ 71 years earlier. The Stringer organ was one of power and sweetness. It was first used on 18th May 1870, followed by an organ recital just one week later. The wind operation was still mechanical but it was in the life-time of this instrument, in September 1926, that Walker and Watson installed a No 13 Discus Electric Blower at a cost of £118 [about £8,000 today].

6.4 Musical festivals at All Saints (1788-1831)

In September 1788 it was decided to hold a Grand Music Festival in Derby. The feast of music was planned to take place over three days. The festival opened with a performance of the *Messiah* at All Saints Church on the first day. On the second day, the venue for the music moved to The Theatre which was in Bold Lane. Then on the third and final day there was a concert of sacred music at All Saints Church. One can only assume that the Smith organ, then about 85 years old was performing reliably. We know of course that it was worn out by 1807. Costs for the festival were high because many of the musicians who were to participate were distinguished performers. For this reason tickets were quite expensive. Tickets for the Grand Music Festival [the three days] were priced at one guinea (£1 1s 0d) [about £250 today] and so one can appreciate the slight nervousness of those who wondered whether the Festival would attract a good-sized audience – especially as this was the first such occasion at Derby. However, the fears were not realised. The tickets were over subscribed. One thousand people crowded into All Saints for the *Messiah* and the event was a major success and another Grand Music Festival was held in 1793.

There were more concerts in the early years of the 19th century. Music Festivals were organised to raise funding for the building of the General Infirmary in Full Street. The first festival was held in 1810, which was of course just two years after the installation of the new Eliot organ at All Saints. There is no doubt that acquisition of this fine instrument was a key factor in the decision to organise concerts.

All inclusive tickets for the event were five guineas (£5 5s 0d) [about £800 today] but despite this high price the festivals were clearly a success and were held regularly every three

years until 1831. Thus the years between 1788 and 1831 were a golden period for music festivals with All Saints Church making a major contribution. By the late 19th century, the opening of the church for events other than services for Christian worship, even if the purpose was to listen to sacred music for charitable purposes, was frowned upon.

6.5 The east wall and the memorial windows

The first record that we have regarding the decoration of the east wall behind the altar is the installation of a large semi-circular painting in 1807. The oil painting by James Rawlinson was titled *The Visit of the Three Maries to the Empty Tomb*. The three Maries may be Mary mother of Jesus, Mary Magdalene and Mary mother of James but it is not easy to reconcile the title of the painting with the gospel accounts. In St Mark's Gospel [16.v1], Mary mother of James, Mary Magdalene *and Salome* set out to visit the grave and anoint the body. In the picture, the three women approach an angel who occupies the centre of the picture. To the right of a tree, several tomb guards are in slumber (Fig. 6.7).

Figure 6.7: An engraving of the painting titled *The Visit of the Three Maries to the Empty Tomb* by James Rawlinson. The work was mounted behind the altar between 1807 and 1863. From Cox & Hope (1881).

In 1861, Prince Albert, the beloved consort of Queen Victoria died unexpectedly when he succumbed to an infection contracted after being out in poor weather. The nation was saddened by the loss of this energetic patron of the Arts and at All Saints it was agreed to commission Clayton and Bell to design, make and install three stained glass windows, as a memorial to Prince Albert, in the upper part of the east wall behind the altar (Fig. 6.8).

In 1863, the painting by James Rawlinson was taken down and the stained glass artwork was installed. A tall central window with a rounded head depicted *The Crucifixion* while the smaller rectangular windows on each side showed *The Adoration of the Magi* [left] and *Baptism in the River Jordan* [right]. The cost of the artwork and installation was £700 (about £100,000 today) and was funded by public subscription.

6.6 The church interior in early Victorian times

The Victorian period ushered in fresh thinking in the Church of England on how church interiors should be organised and how churches should be made more beautiful. Required by Royal Order (1561) chancel screens served an important function. They were not, as one might first suppose, installed to mark a line of separation between the areas occupied by the laity and the clergy. Rather, the chancel screen identified the protected area where laity and clergy together could be in Communion with God during the celebration of the Eucharist.

During the 19th century chancel screens fell out of favour. They tended to obscure views of the chancel and the altar and so they were reduced or removed from many churches.

Figure 6.8: A colour lithograph of the Prince Albert Memorial Window which replaced the painting of *The Visit of the Three Maries to the Empty Tomb* in the east wall behind the altar. Three large windows were fitted with stained glass. In the centre *The Crucifixion* occupied the tallest window which had a rounded head. The window to the left of the *Crucifixion* was smaller and showed *The Adoration of the Magi;* while the window on the right showed *Baptism in the River Jordan.* The pictures are in the Italian Early Renaissance style but curiously the colour blue is absent. The windows were designed by Clayton and Bell and installed in memory of Prince Albert in 1863. The windows have been represented here at the same size to enable the reader to see the images clearly. The windows were dismantled in order to facilitate the Cathedral east end extension completed in 1972. From Cox & Hope (1881).

By the beginning of Victorian times, the chancel screen at All Saints had been greatly reduced. The central section was removed altogether. By 1849, the central section of the chancel screen was reinstated as we see in the engraving by N Rowbottom in the same year (Fig. 6.3). However, the reinstated screen was positioned close to the east end of the Church, crossing the main aisle by the first pair of columns from the east wall. The chancel screen had therefore moved forward and now defined the sanctuary (Fig. 6.9).

The engraving by Rowbottom also shows that there was a problem with the capacity of the church for the congregation. The main aisle is occupied by a cohort of at least 14 benches each of which could take five people. Thus there was seating for at least 70 additional people in the main aisle. It is noteworthy that this provision of additional capacity was still necessary after the completion of new galleries at the west end on the north and on the south sides of the church in 1841.

The Church - 1849

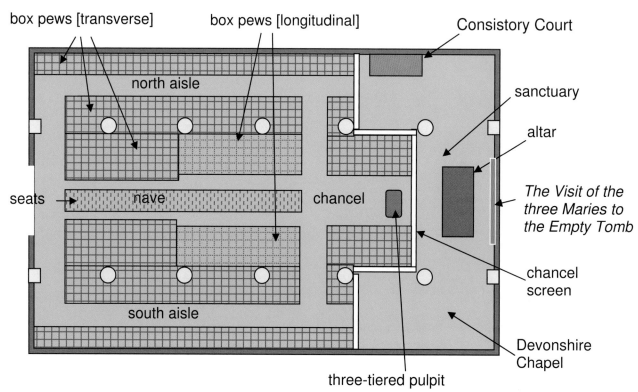

Figure 6.9: A schematic plan view of the church in early Victorian times based upon the information in the engraving by N Rowbottom (1849). While most box pews were orientated transverse to the east-west axis of the church, the pews adjacent to the main aisle in the middle of the nave were orientated longitudinally. The screen was positioned between the first pair of columns immediately in front of the sanctuary. PHB

6.7 The major re-ordering in 1873

During the mid-1850s The Revd Edward Walwyn Foley, minister at All Saints from 1849 to 1871, developed elaborate plans to enhance the beauty of the church. He wanted to replace all the box pews with bench pews and thereby increase the capacity of the church. He planned to remove the wrought iron screen in order to make more room for seating in the chancel. In refinements intended to increase the beauty of the church, he wished to replace the plain glass of the aisle windows with coloured glass and build a grand marble reredos behind the altar.

A number of influential people were concerned about the proposed removal of Bakewell's beautiful wrought iron screen. They pressed

The 18th century three-tier pulpit was placed in a central position at the front of the nave where it had been first positioned about 100 years earlier. This enabled the majority of the congregation to see the minister during the sermon, except those whose seats in the box pews were facing west. However, this position occluded the altar and so we find that by the end of the 19th century the pulpit had been moved to the north of the nave.

their case for the retention of the screen and the matter was taken to the Consistory Court at Lichfield.

In a compromise agreement, the screen would be retained but the side railings and gates of the Devonshire Chapel and the vestry would be re-located to the north and south sides respectively of the sanctuary. This would have resulted in placing an ironwork screen around three sides of the sanctuary making the area resemble a cage. In the actual re-ordering, the agreement was not honoured. A contemporary engraving of the church interior shows that the central section of the chancel screen survived; but the Bakewell aisle and parclose screens and gates were removed completely (Figs.6.10 & 6.11). Sadly, it later proved impossible to re-instate the original ironwork.

Figure 6.10: A view of the interior of the church engraved after the re-ordering of 1873. Only the central section of the screen survived. The main aisle is occupied by a cohort of seats. From Cox & Hope (1881).

The re-ordering proceeded in 1873, shortly after The Revd Foley left his position as minister. All the 18th century box pews were replaced by bench pews resulting in a welcome increase in seating capacity but it still proved necessary to place additional seating in the main aisle (Figs. 6.10 & 6.11). The problem of limited capacity for the congregation was not resolved until the Cathedral Church was enlarged almost a century later in 1972.

The Church - 1873

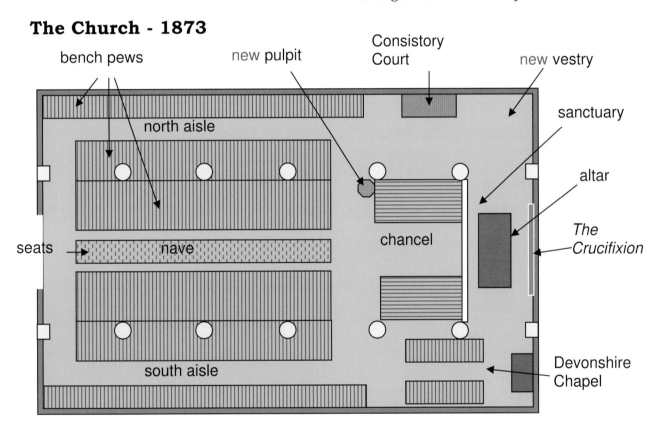

Figure 6.11: A schematic plan of the church following the major re-ordering completed in 1873. In order to increase capacity bench pews replaced the original box pews. In addition, the aisle screens and parclose screens between the chancel aisles and chancel were removed. A new pulpit was installed and the 16th century oak altar replaced the 1725 marble altar. In addition, a large vestry was built on the north-east corner of the Church.

The plain glass in the large windows of the north and south aisles was replaced with stained glass thereby making the natural lighting in the church more subdued.

The 1725 three-tier pulpit was replaced by a new oak pulpit designed by Temple Moore. The pulpit, which continues to be used today, rests on a stone base which takes the form of a Corinthian capital with volutes and *Acanthus* leaves. Stone steps with handrail lead up to the pulpit (Fig. 6.12). There was no canopy or sounding board in 1873. A photograph of the interior in 1910 appears to show the sounding

board, but it is not present in illustrations showing the interior in 1927 and 1934. The contemporary engraving (Fig. 6.12) shows the pulpit in a central aisle position but in order to prevent the pulpit from obscuring the congregation's view of the altar, it was moved to the north side of the main aisle, positioned by the second column where it remains today.

The lessons were read from a reading desk positioned immediately in front of the pulpit. The reading desk was replaced by the brass lectern which was donated by the husband of Catherine Orme who died in 1891.

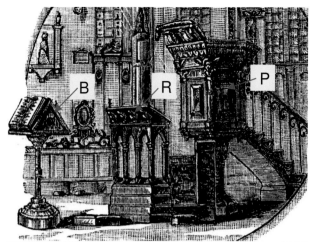

Figure 6.12: An engraving dating from about 1880 shows the new pulpit [P], the reading desk [R] and a Bible stand [B] all clustered in the centre of the chancel. From Cox & Hope (1881).

Robert Bakewell's beautiful wrought ironwork appeared to be under sustained attack. In addition to the major reduction of the chancel screen, the 1725 Duke's Red marble-top altar supported by a fine ironwork base was replaced by the 1620 oak altar which had been stored in the vestry. The vicar The Revd S D C Douglas had the marble inscribed at length to the effect that its use as an altar (1725-1873) had been 'inappropriate' but this was not the case. Robert Bakewell's ironwork base now resides in the Cavendish Area fitted with a later Sicilian Pencil Vein marble top.

Outside the church, Robert Bakewell's fine entrance gates were sold and the boundary railings were replaced. The new railings were quite ornate with a repeated quatre-foil-in-a-circle design along the length of the railings (Fig. 6.13). They survived until World War II.

Figure 6.13: Detail of part of an engraving of All Saints Church viewed from the west following road widening in 1873. Elegant new railings and gates replaced Robert Bakewell's original ironwork. Note delicate ornamental design [arrow]. The south aisle door is seen behind the gates. From Derby Cathedral Official Guide (1972).

The entire cost of the 1873 re-ordering is recorded at the exceedingly precise figure of £5,991 6s 1d [about £720,000 today].

6.8 Repairs to the 18th century church building

The parish accounts show that significant repairs were necessary from the middle part of the 18th century. In 1769 and in 1782, it was necessary to repave areas of the church floor. The central aisle had to be repaved in 1826. The church also needed to be repainted every thirty to forty years during the 19th century. In 1826, the church was painted throughout to imitate stonework with the exception of the ceilings which were white washed. The following year attention turned to the columns and railings. In 1848 there was cleaning and more painting with special attention to the wrought iron screen, particularly gilding the Royal Arms, the railings and the gates. The whole church was repainted again at the time of the 1873 re-ordering and again in 1904/5.

There was extensive restoration of the interior and exterior of the entire church in 1904/5. Scaffolding was erected over the entire edifice to facilitate extensive cleaning and restoration of the stonework. Inside the church a new carved oak panel delimited the chancel choir stalls (Fig. 6.14).

Figure 6.14: Carved *Acanthus* leaf decoration on one of the chancel oak panels installed in 1905. The panel is about 45 cm wide. PHB

In the sanctuary new white marble paving was also laid at this time. The cost of the major restoration of 1904/5 was £10,000 [about £1 million today]. Three members of the Evans family were generous benefactors who contributed to the cost of the panel and the marble paving. Sadly, all three died in 1903/4 and were unable to see the new works which were completed in 1905.

7: The raising to Cathedral status and the east end extension

7.1 The diocesan history of All Saints Church

From the time of its establishment in 943 until 1884, a period of 941 years, All Saints Church was located within the Diocese of [Coventry and] Lichfield. As we saw in Chapter 2, the relationship had been strained because All Saints had been designated a Royal Free Chapel. For the first circa 160 years, it had been an *independent* Royal Free Chapel, but after 1107 it had belonged to the Dean and Chapter of Lincoln Cathedral. Successive kings of England had made it perfectly clear that All Saints was not subject to the normal episcopal control and bishops of the Diocese could not make formal visitations. However, they could hold ordinations and clearly did. The distancing from bishops continued after the Reformation when, in 1555, Queen Mary gave the power to appoint ministers to the bailiffs and burgesses of Derby.

However, these powers were terminated in 1838, and in 1884 All Saints Church was included in the new Diocese of Southwell. In recognition of its importance within the Diocese, Suffragan Bishops of Derby were appointed from the early part of the 20th century. The relationship between All Saints Church Derby and the Southwell Diocese was a much happier one than had been the case historically and there also seems to have been an appreciation that at some date Derby would become a separate diocese.

7.2 All Saints becomes a Cathedral Church

In August 1927, it was formally announced that there was to be a Diocese of Derby. None of the churches in Derbyshire was ideally suited for designation as a Cathedral because they all had limited capacity to host large ceremonial events. Some thought St Werburgh - beautifully rebuilt in 1894 - would be chosen but it was decided to make All Saints the Cathedral Church. Henceforth, the church would *welcome* the presence of the bishop.

The church was hallowed as the Cathedral Church of All Saints Derby on 27th October 1927 and Dr Edmund Pearce was enthroned the following day. A special book on the See of Derby was published in celebration of the event. In preparation for the hallowing there was significant re-ordering. The central section of the chancel screen was moved to its original 1725 position enclosing the Temple Moore choir stalls installed in 1894 (Figs. 7.1 & 7.3).

Figure 7.1: The chancel screen reinstated in its 1725 position. Note the tester [arrow]. From Eeles 1934.

7.3 The Greek Orthodox Cathedra

The formal relationship between All Saints and the Diocese was transformed. In the past, All Saints had been ambivalent about the presence of the diocesan bishop in any formal capacity. From 27th October 1927, All Saints had the honour, privilege and duty to provide a cathedra [seat] for the bishop. The seat was procured in a most original and delightful way. The Revd Roland Borough, Chaplain of the Crimea Memorial Church in Constantinople from 1910 to 1926, purchased a 16th century Greek Orthodox throne (Fig.7.2) from a Turkish antique shop in Constantinople. The Greek Archbishop Germanos was invited to bless the throne at the hallowing of the Cathedral.

Figure 7.2: The canopy of the 16th century Greek Orthodox cathedra purchased in Constantinople in 1927. Note the embroidery of the coat of arms of the See of Derby produced by the Cathedral Workshop. From Derby Cathedral Official Guide (2014).

The Cathedral Church - 1927

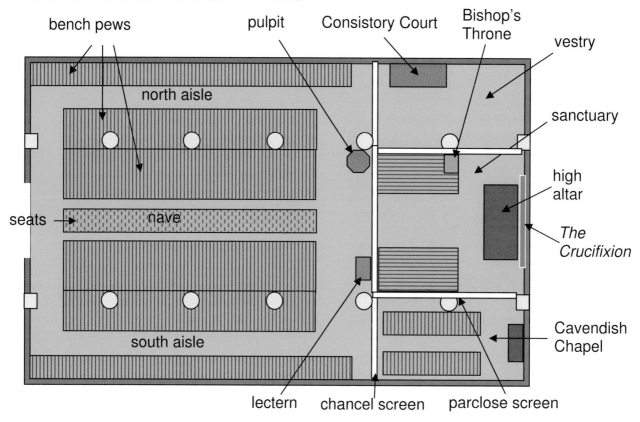

Figure: 7.3: Schematic plan of the Cathedral Church of All Saints on the occasion of the enthronement of the first Bishop of the Diocese: Dr Edmund Pearce on 28th October 1927. Note the reinstated chancel screen. PHB

7.4 The installation of the Compton organ

With the rise in status to Cathedral in 1927, it became imperative that the quality of sacred music provided by the choir and organ was of the highest standard. When Dr G H Heath Gracie came to All Saints in 1933, he was not impressed. He referred to the wreck of the once fine Stringer instrument which faced him on his arrival. The pipe-work was 'lamentable'. There was also another problem. Since 1894, the choir had moved from the galleries to the choral stalls in the chancel and he found the remoteness of the choir from the organ intolerable. So it was time for another organ committee. This was established in 1934 and by 1938 a contract had been given to John Compton Organ Company Ltd.

It had been hoped to reuse the 1703 organ casing for a fourth time, but when it was dismantled it was found to be in very poor condition – held together by softwood riddled with wood worm. The new instrument had 2,800 pipes which required protection from the noxious fumes now wafting across Full Street from the neighbouring power station. It was decided to enclose the pipes in three large swell boxes. The old casing was stored with the vain

hope that it could be used again, but it rotted away during the Second World War.

The Compton organ reused 1,535 pipes from the Stringer organ, hence more than half of the pipes in the new organ were recycled. The console featured illuminated stops of the push button type. The cost of the new organ was £3,600 [about £220,000 today]. Eventually, in 1963, the unsightly swell boxes which held all the pipes together were hidden by a gothic style screen of dummy pipes designed by Sebastian Comper.

7.5 The Ceri Richards windows

In 1953, Ronald Beddoes (1912-2000) was appointed Provost of the cathedral, a position which he served with distinction for 27 years. He was a man of energy with considerable management skills. During the 1950s the fabric was discoloured with grime from the dust-laden factory air and the Cathedral capacity was still insufficient. He resolved to address these problems and improve the cathedral support for the community. In 1965 he commissioned Ceri Richards (1903–1971) to design a pair of stained glass windows for the east end of the north and south aisles. The abstract designs represent the intensity of the battle between light and dark (Fig. 7.4).

Figure 7.4: The north and south aisle east windows designed by Ceri Richards (1965). From Derby Cathedral Official Guide (2014).

The north window, dominated by deep blues with a few flashes of yellow, represents the dark forces - All Souls. The south window is dominated by yellow and signifies the triumph of light over darkness – All Saints.

7.6   The 1968-1972 Cathedral extension

All Saints Church had always been too small to accommodate the congregations expected for major occasions. During the 1930s, Sir Ninian Comper had drawn up a plan for a major extension at the east end incorporating a dome and transepts. This would have radically altered the church realised by James Gibbs and there was also a question regarding affordability. The Second World War intervened and the plans were placed in abeyance.

In the mid 1950s Ronald Beddoes engaged the services of Sebastian Comper who reworked his father's plans and produced a classical design which would enhance and complement, rather than overwhelm, the existing James Gibbs building (Figures 7.5 and 7.6).

The Cathedral Church – 1972/3

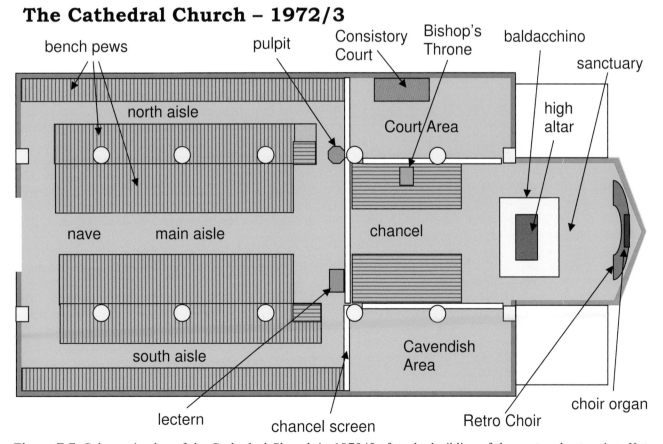

Figure 7.5: Schematic plan of the Cathedral Church in 1972/3 after the building of the east end extension. Note the new Retro Choir with the choir organ which was added in 1973. The altar was no longer placed against the east wall but was positioned in the centre of the sanctuary under a classical Roman style baldacchino. St Katharine's Chapel is located under the west part of the Cavendish Area and chancel. PHB

Sebastian Comper produced a classical design that complemented the 1725 James Gibbs building. The creation of an extension at the east end enabled the choir to move from the choir stalls in the chancel to a Retro-Choir behind the altar as seen for example at Westminster Cathedral. This increased the space available to accommodate large numbers of clergy who participate in special services and also increased flexibility in the use of the space. A further advantage of creating a Retro-Choir was that it avoided the need for the sanctuary to move eastwards, becoming more remote from the congregation (Fig. 7.5).

Figure 7.6: A drawing by Sebastian Comper of his plan for the east extension of The Cathedral Church. The upper level accommodates the Retro-Choir [arrow]. The lower level includes the vestry, Chapter room, meeting rooms and Song Room. From Derby Cathedral Guide (1972).

Soon after the completion of the extension in early 1972, it was realised that the problem of time differential between the choir and organ sound had worsened. It was very difficult to accompany the choir with the Compton organ when the choir occupied the Retro-Choir. On occasions it was necessary to accompany the choir on a piano, an unusual scenario in a cathedral.

The solution was very simple. In 1973 a small two-manual Cousans organ, shaped like a swallow-tail, was installed in the middle of the Retro-Choir. This instantly addressed the problem. The new organ was adorned with two cherubs – the only survivors from the Smith organ casing of 1703 (Fig. 7.7).

A three-seat sedilia was installed in memory of the first Bishop of Derby, Dr Edmund Pearce. Unusually, the sedilia which provides formal seating for the officiating clergy, is carved in oak rather than stone and is placed against the *north* rather than the south wall of the chancel.

Figure 7.7: The two gilded cherubs rescued from the casing of the Bernard Smith organ made in 1703. They now decorate the Cousans choir organ. Clearly they mourn the loss of the Smith organ casing. PHB

7.7 The building of a baldacchino

As a major feature in the new sanctuary, Sebastian Comper designed an elegant classical baldacchino which he positioned over the altar. The baldacchino comprises four non-fluted Corinthian columns supporting a lower cornice. A colonnade of colonnettes springs up from the lower cornice on all four sides to support a raised pedimented canopy.

This raised pediment design has the pleasing effect of allowing light to stream from the windows around the Retro-Choir directly into the upper part of the baldacchino, thereby increasing the intensity of the daylight above the altar. Sebastian Comper also took a gilded tester designed by his father, which hitherto had been suspended above the altar (Fig. 7.1), and integrated it into the ceiling of the baldacchino. The classical Roman design of the baldacchino perfectly complements the Roman Baroque design of the James Gibbs church.

7.8 The loss of the 1863 memorial windows

At the lower ground level beneath the sanctuary and Retro-Choir, Comper planned a new vestry, Chapter room, meeting rooms and a choir Song Room. The implementation of Sebastian Comper's design involved the demolition of the large 1873 vestry and, sadly, the dismantling of the 1863 Prince Albert memorial windows. It is thought that the coloured glass was stored in St Katharine's Chapel for a while but it was eventually sold.

8: The bells, the clock and the carillon

8.1 The Bell Chamber and the bells

The Cathedral Church of All Saints has the oldest ring of ten bells in the world. All of the bells are at least 300 years old and all except one have been in the tower since the late 17th century (Fig. 8.1).

Figure 8.1: The ring of ten bells with their stocks and wheels mounted on the 1927 iron frame. They are arranged in a clockwise spiral starting with the Treble (No 1) on the lower left. The Tenor (No 10), the largest bell, is seen to the centre right. From the Derby Cathedral Official Guide (2014).

Bells are normally numbered in order of increasing weight. The lightest bell is known as the treble and the heaviest is known as the tenor. The earliest information that we have indicates that the bells were rung in 1510. There were only four bells at that time and they were presumably in a temporary home because All Saints did not have a tower at that time. Construction work was just commencing on the new tower in 1510. The ring is thought to have increased to five bells when the tenor bell transferred from Dale Abbey during the Reformation period. This is the oldest as well as the heaviest bell. It is thought to date from about 1520 and it weighs 1.6 tonnes.

A sixth bell was added in 1620 and is known as the Batchelor's Bell because it was partially funded by bachelors in Derby who raised £15 16s 2d towards the total cost of £33 1s 6d. The cost of a new bell covered the manufacture of the bell, the transport of the bell to Derby and then the raising of the bell in the tower and fixture to the bell frame. The other bells which formed part of the ring in the early 16th century were recast or replaced during the 17th century.

In 1677 four more bells were procured through the efforts of Francis Thacker, Church Warden, and increased the ring to ten bells. The four new bells were initially mounted above the existing set. However, in July 1687, it was noted that the wooden frame and bell wheels which were in the order of 150 years old, were decayed and beyond repair. It was decided to re-hang all the bells at one level on a new wooden frame built by John Baxter of Laxton, Northampton. The frame was installed by George Sorocold, church warden and engineer.

The striking of the bells produces very considerable downward and lateral stresses in a bell tower and so the bell frame and tower must be extremely robust. The major installation, which cost £37 16s 2d (£37.81), [about £37,000 today] was very successful. This 17th century wooden frame lasted 240 years until 1927 when the bells were re-hung onto a cast iron frame with cast iron head stocks and ball-bearings. The work was done by Taylors shortly before All Saints was hallowed as a Cathedral in October 1927.

The most recent arrival is a bell, cast in 1632 and formerly a member of a ring of six bells at Ashbourne Church. Early in 1712, the 8th bell at All Saints became cracked. The Church Wardens made an agreement with John Halton that his bother Emmanuel Halton would recast it. There was a long delay but eventually the bell was recast for around £7 and re-hung for a further 5s 0d (25p). Just over one hundred years later in 1815, Ashbourne Church suffered a cracked tenor bell. Rather than recast the bell, it was decided to replace the ring of six bells with a new ring of eight bells.

The original ring was removed by William Dobson of Downham Market, Norfolk who supplied a new ring of eight bells to Ashbourne Church in October 1815. A swap at All Saints Church was now arranged. The old 5th bell at Ashbourne was procured by All Saints Church from William Dobson in exchange for the recast 1712 bell. Thus the 8th bell at All Saints is a former member of the Ashbourne Church ring. The fate of the ejected 1712 bell is unknown.

The level at which the bells were fixed oscillated during the first 150 years of the life of the present tower. At first in 1532, the bells were fixed at a lower level than today. They were raised to the present level early in the 17th century. The bells then returned to the original level in 1665 before being raised again to the current level in 1687 where they have remained. Until 1666 the bell ringing loft was positioned at the level of the West Window sill and was separated by railings from the contemporary gallery in the mediaeval church. However, in that year the bell ringing loft was moved up to its present position in the second storey.

8.2 The inscriptions on the bells

Each bell bears an inspirational inscription engraved in a band positioned just below the shoulder of the bell. The lettering is either in lombardic or in Roman font. Errors such as the misspelling of names, the inversion of letters and the transposition of numerals are quite common despite the permanence and importance of the inscriptions. Examples of the ornamental inscriptions are shown in Figure 8.2.

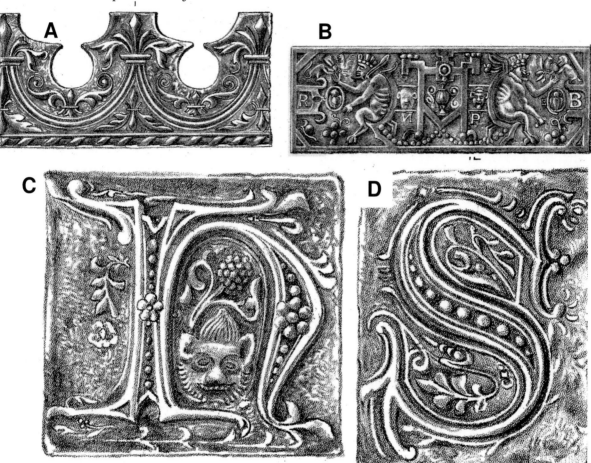

Figure 8.2: Ornamental features on the 17th century bells recorded as rubbings by J Bailey circa 1880. A - The ornament inserted between each word of the inscription on the second bell (1687 or 1678); B - The ornament in between the words of the inscription on the Batchelor's Bell (1620); C and D - Ornamental lombardic capitals on the sixth bell (1607). From Cox & Hope (1881).

In Table 8.1 the bells of the ring of ten are listed in order commencing with the lightest (Treble) and finishing with the heaviest (Tenor). The Table includes the date of casting and the diameter of each bell at the lip of the sounding bow. The inscription on each bell and any other engraved letters or images are also listed.

8.3   Bell repairs

Though seemingly robust, bells suffer damage over long periods of time or from inexperienced bell ringers. Bells can become cracked or indented which adversely affects the striking note and the partial tones of the bell. Minor problems can be rectified by turning the bell by one quarter of a turn but a cracked bell needs to be recast or replaced at considerable expense. There are numerous records of repairs to the bells in the 17th century. A minor repair to one bell in 1623 cost just 4d (2p) but trussing and mending a bell wheel in 1630 cost £1 3s 2d (£1.16). In 1670 Josiah Wheeldon was paid £3 3s 8d (£3.18) for a series of repairs to the bells.

8.4   Bell ringing and the bell ringers

The records show that in the 17th century the bells were rung each day at particular times to inform those without clocks of prescient activities.

44

Bell	Maker & Date	Diameter	Inscription in band positioned just below shoulder of bell
1st treble	1678	0.73 m	GOD SAVE HIS CHURCH FRA THACKER I RAGG 1678 The lettering is in lombardic capital. The bell was made by William Noone of Nottingham.
2nd	1678	0.75 m	GOD SAVE HIS CHURCH 1687 F THACKAR AND G SARACOLE The lettering is in Roman Capitals. The last two digits of the date have been transposed; the date of casting was 1678. The two names are also misspelt. They should read **F THACKER** and **G SOROCOLD**. The bell was made by William Noone of Nottingham.
3rd	1693	0.85 m	LET DABY BEE EVER HAPPY NAT PRIME THO CHAPMN WARDENS 1693 The lettering is in lombardic font except **WARDENS** which is in Roman font. The letter R is missing from **DARBY** and the letter A is missing from **CHAPMAN**. The bell was made by William Noone of Nottingham.
4th	1677	0.83 m	**COELVM REMUNERET BENEFACTORIBUS MEIS** (May Heaven reward my benefactors). This was probably one of the new bells installed in 1676-7. The bell was made by Daniel Hedderley.
5th	1620	0.9 m	**BATCHELERS BELL 1620** The lettering is in Roman Capitals. The **B** of **BELL** is inverted. Ornaments of satyrs, monkeys and squirrels and an owl of Minerva are placed between the words. The letters **R N P B** are also engraved but it is not known to what they refer. The mark of George Oldfield, the Bell Founder in Nottingham who cast the bell is on the waist of the bell.
6th	1607	1.0 m	HEE CAMPANA SAERA FIAT TRINITATE BEATA 1607 (May this bell be blessed by Holy Trinity). The initials IB RP HO HB GB TW are inscribed on the waist of the bell. These may stand for Edward Bennett (vicar), RP Robert Parr, (Church Warden), HD (not HO) Henry Deane, HB Henry Bingham, GB Gabriel Barber or George Blagreave (Sexton). Until 1677 this was the second bell. The bell was made by Henry Oldfield of Nottingham.
7th	1629	1.08 m	**NON NOBIS DOMINE NUTV NOBIS SED NOMENS TVO DA GORIAN E WIS 1629** (Not unto us O Lord not with us but to Thy Name give us glory). The lettering is in Roman Capitals except the initials which are lombardic. On the waist the letters **GB** probably refer to George Blagreave, the Sexton. The bell was cast by George Oldfield in Nottingham and was the 3rd bell in the ring of six until 1677. There were many repairs to this bell between 1636 and 1670.
8th	1632	1.10 m	GOD SAVE THE CHUKCH 1632 There are two errors in the inscription. The letter K should be the letter R and the second C of **CHURCH** is inverted. This bell was the 5th bell in the ring of six at Ashbourne Church until 1815 when it was replaced and then acquired by All Saints. This bell replaced a 17th century bell which had cracked and been recast in 1712. The bell was made by George Oldfield of Nottingham.
9th	1655	1.15 m	**GLORY BE TO GOD ON HIGH 1655** The bell was cast by George Oldfield of Nottingham.
10th tenor	1520	1.28 m	TRINITATE SED HAT BEE CAMPANA BEATA (May this bell be blessed by the Holy Trinity). This bell was made by the Seliok family in Nottingham.

Table 8.1: A list of the ring of ten bells at the Cathedral Church of All Saints Derby and their dates, makers and inscriptions. Information from Cox & Hope (1881) and Halls and Dawson (1998).

The bell at 05.00 served to inform travellers and labourers that it was time to rise. A single bell would be tolled at 07.00 and two bells at 08.00. In the evening, a bell was rung at 20.00. These bell ringing times were traditional and probably dated from before the Reformation. During the 19th century, bell ringing during the day was progressively reduced.

In addition to the bell ringing to call the faithful for church services, the bells were rung on days of national and local importance. These included the triennial visitation by the bishop, the anniversary of the failure of the Gunpowder Plot on 5th November 1605, St George's Day on 23rd April, the Royal Oak Day on 29th May, the king's birthday, the annual perambulation of the parish boundary and the anniversary of various important battles. In addition the bells were rung to celebrate new victories or the death of major national figures. The accounts show that during the 17th century, the bell ringers were paid on each occasion collective amounts typically ranging from one shilling to ten shillings (5p to 50p) [about £50 to £500 today]. There was a constant need to supply candle wax to provide light for the bell ringers. At that time the cost was about 2s 6d (13p) for six pounds of wax.

On 12th February 1722, six days before the unapproved demolition of the mediaeval church building, there was a parish order that the bells should be rung at the usual times for the All Saints parishioners to meet *in St Michael's Church* until further notice. This does appear to give a heavy hint of what was planned.

There are also records of some 18th and 19th century bell peals. A peal is defined as over 5,000 changes in the sequence of bells rung in each round. Normally, all except the 8th and 9th bells are included in the peal. On Tuesday 15th February 1763 the *Peal of Grandsire Triples* was undertaken. This required 5,040 changes and took just under three hours and eight minutes. On 24th January 1805, the *Holt Peal of Grandsire Triples*, with the same number of changes, was completed in three hours and 55 minutes. Twenty-one years later an *Abstract of a Peal of Bob Major*, again with 5,040 changes, was performed for the first time on 18th March 1826. Four years later the Derby Society of Change Ringers performed the first *Peal of Grandsire Cators*, involving 5,093 changes, was completed in three hours and 42 minutes. This was the greatest number of changes performed with these bells and all ten bells were used.

In the early part of the 20th century there were concerns about the robustness of the tower and the bell frame and so peals were rare. A peal was performed in 1912 and the next one was fifteen years later, after the replacement of the 17th century bell frame in 1927. After the designation of All Saints as a Cathedral Church, bell ringing assumed greater importance. James Pagett was appointed as the first Cathedral Ringing Master. He was a stocky man and very fit. On one occasion he managed to play the 9th bell and the tenor at the same time. He held the position as Ringing Master until his death in 1947.

Since 1927 the Derby Cathedral bell ringers have performed many peals each decade including Grandsire Doubles, Grandsire Triples, Grandsire and Stedman Caters, Plain Bob, Cambridge, New Cambridge, Yorkshire Surprise, London Surprise Major and many others. The Cathedral band is frequently joined by experienced guest bell ringers. It has won the Horsley Cup – a competition for advanced bands in the Diocese - many times.

8.5 The story of the clock

How long has there been a clock on the tower? Was there a clock in the tower when it was first built? The Parish accounts make reference to a payment for the repair of the clock in 1575, so it is likely that a clock was installed when the new tower was completed in 1532 although there is no direct evidence of this. The records inform us that there have been four clocks in the lifetime of the tower to date and the clock dial has moved up to its present position.

The earliest clock was positioned much lower than it is today. It had just one exterior dial - displayed on the west face of the tower above the West Door, immediately below the base of the West Window. However, this clock also had an *interior* dial in the nave which could be seen by people in the church. Numerous 17th century repairs and improvements are recorded.

In 1633, a new clock-house was constructed for £2 and in the same year, new wheels were fitted to the clock for a further £2. A reference to repairing the chimes in 1657 indicates that the clock did chime the hours from at least the mid-17th century. Then in 1679, machinery was installed for striking the quarter-hour. The church wardens paid £2 to the sexton, J Ragg, for this improvement.

By 1732, the original clock was beyond further repair and in August 1732 it was removed. George Ashmore was paid the sum of £8 8s 0d (eight guineas) [about £8,000 today] by the church wardens for a new clock. At this time there were plans to build a gallery at the west end to house an organ and so there was no longer any possibility of an interior clock dial. Hence the Ashmore clock was installed in a new clock-house which was positioned near the base of the second stage of the tower.

Despite initial optimism, it was only a few years before the new clock needed major work. The Ashmore clock was greatly altered, or superseded, by a clock mechanism installed by John Whitehurst in 1745. This third clock was a four-day clock with three-wheel train and dead-beat pin-wheel escapement invented by Whitehurst. The pendulum was five metres in length with a beat every two seconds. The clock triggered a hammer to strike the tenor bell to sound the hour. The quarters were sounded by the third and sixth bells. Large exterior clock dials, 3 metres in diameter, were installed on the west and south faces of the tower in the positions where we see them today. John Whitehurst's clock served 182 years before the clock mechanism was replaced by John Smiths of Derby in 1927. The bar which drives the clock hands was discovered to be the barrel of a 1745 carbine adapted for the purpose by John Whitehurst. The barrel was found to be serviceable and with some restoration continued in its role.

Figure 8.3: The clock dial on the south face of the Cathedral tower. The small window with the central mullion above the dial feeds light to the bell ringing loft. The small rectangular windows [arrows] light the spiral stair case to the roof of the tower. PHB

More improvements followed. In 1964, new clock dials, 2.4 metres in diameter, were fitted. Twelve years later in 1976, came the most significant advance of all when John Smith installed automatic electrical winding gear for the clock and carillon. Hitherto, twice each week for the previous 240 years, clock winders had ascended the tower steps to the second stage clock-house in order to manually wind the clock. This was quite expensive. The savings fully justified the considerable outlay for the new equipment.

8.6   The carillon

The Cathedral bells chime each hour and also sound on the quarter-hour. At three-hour intervals during the day a carillon plays a short piece of music twice. The carillon comprises a metal drum, fitted with cams, juxtaposed to a horizontal array of levers. As the drum slowly rotates, the cams momentarily lift individual levers which pull sharply on stiff metal cables leading to the bell chamber above. These cables trigger hammers which strike the bells in the

order pre-determined by the fixed cams on the drum and play a tune. The drum is designed to play seven tunes and automatically shifts to play a different tune on each day of the week. The system is quite separate from the bell ringing orchestrated from the bell ringing loft below the carillon room.

The origin of the carillon is obscure because it is unclear whether references in records to 'chimes' relate to the hourly chimes of the clock or to tunes played by a carillon. The carillon is thought to have originated in the early 17th century. Then, about a century later in 1712, George Sorocold improved the chimes *and set five tunes.* But we do not know what these tunes were. John Whitehurst fitted new parts to the carillon in 1745 which continued service until 1914 when it was utterly worn out and it fell silent. We know that in 1910, the carillon played seven tunes (Table 8.2).

Sunday	Hanover
Monday	The Lass of Pattie's Mill
Tuesday	The Highland Laddie
Wednesday	The Shady Bowers
Thursday	The National Anthem
Friday	March in Scipio
Saturday	The Silken Garter

Table 8.2: The tunes played by the carillon during the late 19th century and the early 20th century.

Most of the tunes probably post-date 1712. We know that two tunes were added in 1762 at a cost of one guinea [£1.05] and the national anthem was added in 1794.

The Revd Herbert Ham, Vicar of the newly hallowed Cathedral Church, decided to resurrect the carillon. He succeeded and on 7th June 1931 there was a service of dedication for the new carillon installed by John Smith & Sons. The new drum continued the tradition of playing a different tune on each day of the week. The organising committee introduced four hymns and kept three of the old tunes (Table 8.3).

Sunday	All Saints
Monday	*The Lass of Pattie's Mill
Tuesday	*The Highland Laddie
Wednesday	Veni Creator
Thursday	Thaxted
Friday	Truro
Saturday	*The Shady Bowers

Table 8.3: The tunes played by the new carillon installed by John Smith & Sons in 1931. The old tunes which were kept are marked with an asterisk.

9: The Chapel of St Mary-on-the-Bridge

9.1   The purpose of bridge chapels

The Chapel of St Mary-on-the-Bridge (Fig. 9.1) is one of a small number of surviving bridge chapels in England. It is a listed Grade I building. During the mediaeval period, chapels were commonly built on stone bridges carrying important roads across rivers. The chapels were integrated into the design of the bridge. Travellers would usually pay a toll at a gatehouse to cross the bridge; then they could call in to the bridge chapel to pray for safe-keeping on their onward journey. The road and chapel were sometimes very closely juxtaposed. At the bridge chapel at Droitwich, for example, the roadway passed through the chapel and separated the priest from the congregation. In mediaeval England, Derby was an important thoroughfare for people travelling from London to the north; and for those travelling east to Nottingham. Travellers heading to the east used this bridge to cross the river Derwent.

Figure 9.1: The Chapel of St Mary-on-the-Bridge viewed from the south-east. This view shows the extensively restored south wall [left] and the largely original east wall [right]. To the far left one can see the Chapel House which was built in the 17th century; in the background to the right we see the south wall of the bridge which replaced the mediaeval bridge in 1794. The top of an arch which passes under the Chapel is visible at the base of the south wall and remnant stonework of the mediaeval bridge is seen on the lower right. The bridge chapel served travellers during the 14th – 16th centuries until it was closed in 1547. After falling into decay in 19th century, it was restored in 1930-2 and is once more a place of Christian worship. Drawn in June 2014 PHB

9.2   The origin of St Mary-on-the-Bridge

The first bridge chapel at this site is thought to have been ordered by the burgesses of Derby in the late 13th century. The present building was probably built 100 years later in the late 14th century. There was a major phase of building at All Saints Church in the same century. The Chapel was an integral part of a stone bridge which carried the road to Nottingham across the southward flowing river Derwent. An early 18th century engraving (Fig. 9.2) suggests that the bridge was narrow and could only take cart traffic in one direction at a time. The Chapel was built on the west bank of the river Derwent on the south side of the road.

48

The bridge appears to have had seven main arches and an arch which allowed overflow water to pass under the Chapel during flood events. One can also see remnant stonework of the second arch springing from the north-east corner of the Chapel. The east face of the Chapel incorporates large shaped slabs of sandstone which form a feature which projects out towards the river at the high flood level. This robust structure would have protected the Chapel building from the impact of large logs and other floating debris surging downstream during major floods. Although the mediaeval bridge was dismantled in 1789, the base of one pier with five stones still *in situ* can be seen at low water on the west side of the river adjacent to the Chapel. The replacement bridge was completed a few metres upstream from the old one in 1794.

Figure 9.2: Detail of *The East prospect of Derby* by Samuel and Nathaniel Buck (1728) showing St Mary's Bridge carrying the road to Nottingham. The Chapel of St Mary-on-the-Bridge is on the west side [arrow]. The bridge appears to have been only sufficiently wide for single line cart and coach traffic. © November 2014 Derby Museums Trust.

There does not seem to have been a gatehouse. The tolls were collected by a hermit, appointed by the diocesan bishop, who lived in the Chapel and was responsible for its upkeep. The Chapel also had a resident anchoress, Agnes Waly, who was commissioned to serve a solitary life of prayerful silence in her purpose-built cell at the Chapel on 3rd January 1370. The Chapel housed a celebrated statue called the *Black Virgin of Derby* which was a much revered figure. Travellers setting out from Derby would have paid the toll and then entered the Chapel by the north door for mass or prayer. A squint

hole, more properly called a hagioscope (Fig. 9.3) enabled people travelling in an easterly direction to glimpse the sanctuary light. A stone spiral staircase, revealed during the restoration, gave direct access to the river bank from the west end of the Chapel.

Figure 9.3: The north wall of the Chapel showing the squint [hagioscope] (arrow] in a patchwork quilt of masonry resulting from the careful restoration in 1930-2. The dark grey blocks are original. In the 14th century these sandstone blocks would have been pale orange-brown but they have become blackened with grime. Thin terra cotta tiles have been delicately inserted into irregular cavities in the damaged stonework. Large pale-coloured blocks and red bricks have been used to repair larger gaps. PHB

The construction of the bridge and Chapel broadly coincided with a major period of building at All Saints. The east window is the only surviving ecclesiastic feature in the perpendicular style. The window comprises two series of four lights each separated by a mullion. The upper series has cinquefoil heads while the lower series has trefoil heads. The eight lights display blue and yellow stained glass showing aspects of the life of the Virgin Mary. The stained glass was designed by Mary Dobson and installed in 1973, paid for by the friends and relations of Sean Ferguson who had recently died of cancer. In the restoration it was discovered that the original roof was probably made of lead and had a lower pitch than it has today.

The Chapel served in the role of bridge chapel for at least 200 years until all bridge chapels in England were closed in 1547, just two years before the College was dissolved at All Saints Church.

9.3 The Chapel inventory of 1488

The Chapel of St Mary-on-the-Bridge had an early association with All Saints Church. The Church had responsibility for the Chapel in the

15th century and although the Chapel became a secular building in the 18th and 19th centuries it is today once again a Christian building consecrated for worship and under the jurisdiction of the Cathedral Church of All Saints Derby.

An inventory compiled by the church wardens of All Saints Church in 1488 has survived and provides some insight into the contents of the Chapel in the time of Henry VII in the late 15th century. John Dale was the priest at the Chapel. The inventory records one silver gilt chalice, two curettes, one coffer, two tapestry cushions given by Aleson Gonkyn, two velvet hats in blue, two candlesticks and 19 tupers of wax. This inventory dates from a time when All Saints Church was flourishing and was richly decorated.

9.4 The Dissolution and closure

About sixty years later there was dramatic change in fortunes with the Dissolution. The Chapel was closed in 1547 and Christian worship ceased. However, in 1555, Queen Mary gave the building and its contents to the bailiffs and burgesses of Derby (later Derby Corporation) as part of the advowson relating to All Saints Church. This arrangement gave the Corporation rights and resources to perpetuate Christian worship for the community. When she came to the throne, Queen Elizabeth I gifted the Chapel to William Buckley which led to a dispute. Did the building belong to Derby Corporation or to William Buckley? A special Commission was established in 1592 to settle the matter. The Commission concluded that the Chapel and appurtenances belong to the bailiffs and burgesses of Derby Corporation and the letter to William Buckley had no effect.

9.5 The Padley Martyrs

The saddest episode in the history of the Chapel stems from the events of 1588. Nicholas Garlick and Robert Ludham were arrested hiding in a priest's hole at the Fitzherbert's house at Padley near Hathersage. A third priest Richard Simpson was also arrested. On 25th July 1588 these three priests were hung, drawn and quartered at the site of the bridge and their remains were placed on display on the west side of the bridge. This severe and gruesome treatment of three priests, who died for their faith, reflected the deep seated fear of political movements which threatened to take power. There had been plots involving local sympathiser Anthony Babington to put Mary Queen of Scots on the throne and Catholic King Phillip of Spain was preparing a massive sea-borne force to invade England. Mary was executed in 1587 and the Spanish Armada was defeated just a few months after the execution of the Padley Martyrs.

9.6 Varied use in the 17th to 19th centuries

In 1662, Bishop Hackett, whose grandson Dr Michael Hutchinson was to become minister at All Saints Church, granted permission to the Presbyterians to assemble for worship in the Chapel. But in the reign of James II they moved to premises on the east side of Irongate. In the 18th century the Chapel was converted for residential purposes and much of this building work survives today. In the 19th century the Chapel became an engineering workshop which was used for the construction of the pews at the restoration of St Michael's church in 1857.

In 1873, at the time of the major reordering of All Saints Church, the bishop renewed the license for Christian worship at the Chapel. It became a Sunday School and Mission Church for the neighbouring St Alkmund's Church. But in 1912 the Chapel returned to secular use as a workshop and its physical condition worsened.

9.7 The conservational restoration of 1930-2

By the late 1920s, after 380 years of alteration and accelerating decay, the fabric of the former chapel was in an extremely poor condition (Fig.9.4).

Figure 9.4: The south wall of the Bridge Chapel before the restoration (1930-2). Most of this wall and the roof were rebuilt. Note the shed used by the mason Jack Cockayne [left] and the blocks of stone to be recycled from the demolished Exeter Bridge in the foreground [P Hodgson]. Compare this view with Figure 9.1. Photograph courtesy of the Trustees of the Chapel of St Mary-on-the-Bridge. © Society for the Protection of Ancient Buildings.

The south wall of the Chapel had been heavily altered during Georgian and Victorian times. Most of the original masonry in the upper half of the south wall had been replaced during the 19th century with red brick and the original chapel windows had been replaced by rectangular windows. A short flight of steps led to a double doorway giving a south entrance to the contemporary workshop.

Derbyshire Archaeological Society purchased the former Chapel and the house but an appeal for funds for restoration was not successful. However, the family of Sir Alfred Seale Haslam, the former Mayor of Derby, paid for the work in his memory. The painstaking restoration was carried out by Jack Cockayne in 1930-2. The local architects Percy Currey and Charles Thompson directed the restoration and the Society for the Protection of Ancient Buildings provided advice. The north wall of the chapel displays an attractive patchwork of original and restoration masonry (Figs. 9.5 and 9.3).

Figure 9.5: View of the restored north wall and roof of the Bridge Chapel. Note the rough blocks of stone at the base of the wall [RB] overlain by the neatly sawn blocks of blackened original stone [OS]. The position of the squint (Fig. 9.2] is marked [S]. The brick work dates from the 19th and 20th centuries. PHB

At the foot of the north wall, the original rough hewn blocks of stone provide a broad and solid pedestal for the chapel which is separated from the former bank by a low arch. This was originally the first arch of the mediaeval St Mary's Bridge. The stonework of the arch appears restored but many of the other blocks are original.

Higher up the north wall, several courses of the original 14th century neatly cut sandstone blocks survive. Terra cotta tiles were used to infill recesses and crevices in the damaged masonry thereby ensuring that the original 14th century stonework can be clearly identified. There are also neat patches of red brick used for restoration where one or more large blocks of sandstone have decayed or been lost.

In carrying out the restoration of the south wall, the 19th century windows, doorway and brickwork were removed and the upper part of the wall was totally rebuilt using sandstone reclaimed from the former Exeter Bridge which had been replaced. Two sets of mullioned windows with trefoil moulded heads were created and the building was returned to its 14th century appearance. A new roof was necessary. Almost all of the original wooden beams of the roof had rotted away and could not be saved but one mediaeval beam with carved ornamental trefoils has survived and can be viewed from the gallery.

At the commencement of the restoration the interior was severely decayed. The entire floor area and walls had to be reconstructed and redecorated. In addition, a west end gallery was constructed to accommodate a piano.

The Bridge Chapel is administered by the Trustees of the Chapel of St Mary-on-the-Bridge, chaired by the Dean of Derby. The Trustees have forged a close relationship with the Dean and Chapter of the Cathedral and the Bridge Chapel now plays an integral part in the life and service of the Derby Cathedral. Regular services are held at the Bridge Chapel each week. The Russian Orthodox Church also holds services at the Chapel each month and ecumenical services to commemorate the Padley Martyrs and Joan Waste are held annually in late July.

10: Visitors to All Saints through the ages and recent developments

10.1 A long history as a provincial church of significance

As we have seen in the preceding chapters, the Collegiate Church of All Saints had a long history of being at the centre of significant social and historical events in Derbyshire. In the 14th and 15th centuries when the mediaeval church building contained six altars tended by a team of canons and chaplains, there was a constant flow of international visitors rather like a major university today. Derby was a town of some substance throughout the mediaeval period, not least because it was an important staging point for travellers on the north-south and the east-west routes. During the 10th to 12th centuries, Derby was sufficiently important to possess its own mint.

The first record we have of a high profile visitor is in the 13th century. We recall that Henry III came to All Saints in 1267 and on that occasion appointed a new canon to his Royal Chapel (Section 2.2). We have better records of events from the beginning of the 18th century.

10.2 The sermon by Dr Henry Sacheverell

In summer 1709, Dr Henry Sacheverell was invited by his unrelated namesake George Sacheverell, High Sheriff of Derbyshire, to deliver a sermon at All Saints Church. This was not going to be an *ordinary* address. Dr Sacheverell was a prominent Tory critic of the events which had displaced James II from his rightful place on the throne in 1688.

Dr Sacheverell delivered his Sermon on 15th August. He was a handsome, energetic and gifted speaker. His carefully crafted arguments, easy manner, modulated voice and skilled use of invective all enhanced the strength of his case. The sermon was purportedly a discourse on a quotation from the 22nd verse of the 5th Chapter of the First Epistle to Timothy: *"Neither be partakers of other men's sin."* But it was actually a veiled attack on the events which had caused King James II to flee the country in 1688. The clear implication was that James Edward should be the monarch as James III rather than Queen Anne. Members of the Tory gentry and many others in the congregation were sympathetic to the arguments and gave warm and enthusiastic applause.

The thrust of the case presented was highly provocative to the current administration. Prominent members of the Whig Party, then in government, opposed the Jacobite cause. On 5th November, Dr Sacheverell gave another provocative address at St Paul's Cathedral in London. On 15th December the two sermons were the subject of complaint to the House of Commons although the logic of his arguments was perfectly sound. He was then subject to impeachment proceedings in the House of Lords. The trial in Westminster Hall in February 1710 lasted nine days. Dr Sacheverell was found *guilty* of High Crimes and Misdemeanours.

However, there was much public sympathy for the arguments that he had espoused. Even Queen Anne was far from displeased and seemed almost supportive. Consequently, the punishment was [very] light. Dr Sacheverell was suspended from the pulpit for three years and copies of his sermon at All Saints were ordered to be burnt. Many people in London were delighted with the virtual acquittal and when the news reached Derby, there was jubilation. All Saints and other churches rang their bells and bonfires were lit in the Market Place and at Nun's Green.

Queen Anne gave Dr Sacheverell comfortable living at St Andrews in Holborn and the High Sheriff of Derbyshire gave him an estate at Callow near Wirksworth. An election was called and resulted in a Tory administration. This was quite an impact from a single sermon delivered at All Saints Church.

10.3 Bonnie Prince Charlie comes to Derby

In late autumn 1745, HRH Prince Charles Edward Stuart [Bonnie Prince Charlie] marched south from Scotland with his Jacobite army. He planned to enter London, displace the Hanoverian monarch George II from the throne and restore the House of Stuart with himself as King James III. His army captured Carlisle and by December approached Derby from Ashbourne. The Duke of Devonshire had raised a local military force to oppose the army of 7,000, but the defending force made a strategic retreat to Nottingham. The Mayor and other members of the Corporation also absented themselves.

Hence on Wednesday 4th December, the dishevelled and weary army together with about 1,500 non-combatants including the wives of officers sloped into Derby. They walked through Friar Gate and Sadler Gate and gradually assembled in the Market Place during the afternoon. The atmosphere was one of excitement, celebration and anticipation. The Prince arrived in the late afternoon. He was described by sympathisers as charismatic and handsome. There are reports that church bells were rung and there was a proclamation declaring James III to be the King of England.

The Prince made his headquarters in Exeter House in Full Street close to All Saints and billets were found for the soldiers and their retinue.

Figure 10.1: A portrait of HRH Prince Charles Edward Stuart who in 1745 came south with an army of 7,000 in his bid to be crowned King James III. From Derby Cathedral Official Guide (2014).

On the Thursday 5th December, the senior officers visited the local gentry known to be sympathetic to win commitment in the form of resources but little help was forthcoming. On Thursday evening the Prince held a full Council at Exeter House where he was advised that the prospects were not bright. The whole campaign depended upon a bow wave of confidence in the justice and prospective success of the cause. Against his own judgement, he accepted the advice of his senior officers and made the momentous decision to retreat.

We know that on the evening of Thursday 5th December 1745, after the Council decision to retreat had been taken, but before it was promulgated, HRH Prince Charles Edward Stuart came to All Saints Church for Holy Communion. This was a remarkable moment in the history of All Saints Church. The next day the army commenced its retreat and the momentum and confidence in the cause rapidly

ebbed away. He was finally defeated at the battle of Culloden on 16th April 1746. An annual service is held at Derby Cathedral to commemorate the visit of the Prince.

10.4 HM The Queen opens the Cathedral Centre

For many years a local book shop had been based in the building across the road opposite the Cathedral tower. But during the 1990s, the business declined and closed. The Very Revd Michael Perham, Dean of Derby [subsequently Bishop of Gloucester] realised that there was an opportunity to acquire the property and establish a Cathedral Centre. His idea was to set up offices, meeting rooms and a coffee-gift shop which could trade as a commercial business. The profits from the business could then be used to support the Cathedral.

The Cathedral Centre was opened by HM The Queen on the 14th November 2003. The business operation was called Derby Cathedral Enterprises Limited. After a difficult start the commercial operation has consolidated and now flourishes as a Café and a Religious Bookshop which operate together. Bishop A E J Rawlinson (Bishop 1935-1959) founded a Cathedral Library of books on theology, ecclesiastic history and Derbyshire history. This is now housed at the Cathedral Centre.

10.5 The Royal Maundy Service (2010)

Figure 10.2: HM The Queen, HRH Prince Philip, Bishop Alastair Redfern and Acting Dean Elaine Jones are accompanied by the Yeomen of the Guard outside the West Door after the Royal Maundy Service at Derby Cathedral on 1st April 2010.

On 1st April 2010, the Cathedral Church of All Saints Derby was given the great honour of hosting the Royal Maundy Service in which Maundy money was distributed to selected residents of the County. On a cold but bright Spring day, Her Majesty The Queen and HRH The Duke of Edinburgh attended the service and The Queen gave Maundy money to 84 recipients as determined by her age.

10.6 The visit by The Archbishop of Canterbury

In September 2011, Dr Rowan Williams, Archbishop of Canterbury (now Lord Williams) made a visit to the Diocese of Derby. He commenced the event with a visit to the University of Derby where he addressed an invited audience representing interests across the county. The highlight of the visit was the Cathedral Eucharist at the Cathedral where he spoke with many in the congregation after the service.

10.7 Cathedral activities

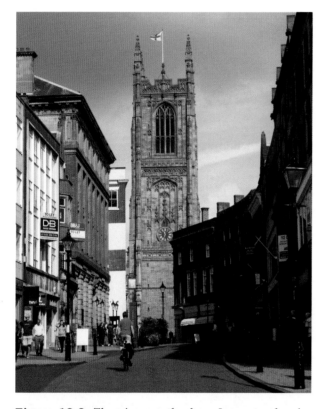

Figure 10.3: The view north along Irongate showing the south face of Derby Cathedral in September 2014. This photograph was taken from a viewpoint close to the one used by Louise Rayner to paint her watercolour [frontispiece] c.150 years earlier. The houses on the east side [right] were set back when they were rebuilt about 1866-1870 in order to widen the street. PHB

In the first few years, there were only three members of Cathedral staff. These were the Revd Herbert Ham, Vicar and Honorary Canon of Derby, the succentor and the reader. Herbert Ham became Provost in 1931. The monthly notes for June 1931 tell of a wide range of Cathedral activities. Following his inspection of Derby All Saints Mixed School the Diocesan Visitor commented: "The opening devotions were very reverently rendered." Meanwhile, the children of Derby All Saints Infants showed a good grasp of what they had been taught. On 6th May 1931, the Bishop confirmed 133 candidates, 23 of whom came from All Saints. The Cathedral Girls' Club gave a concert and raised £2 17s 6d for club activities. The Guilders gave their first concert of songs and satirical sketches on 12th May. One comedian was rated 'quite amusing'. The Duke of Devonshire and the Bishop opened Graeme House for Toc H in Derby.

The Archdeacon of Chesterfield gave a rousing sermon at an open air service [in poor weather] urging Christians to be more cheerful. The Cathedral Cricket team lost to Qualcast but defeated Derby Parks. The Cathedral Choir and bell ringers had a trip to Tewkesbury and Worcester Cathedrals and enjoyed an excellent breakfast, luncheon and a *substantial* tea. In May, 399 visitors went up the tower paying £7 0s 3d [about £400 today]. At Whitsuntide there was a special treat for the children of the two schools who were marched to the Cathedral for a Service. The treat was probably the party and games at Darley Abbey Park afterwards.

In the 1950s and 1960s the Provost Ronald Beddoes brought pastoral flair to the Cathedral and congregations grew. Although he was most at home with liturgy, he became fully involved in the community. In an innovative move, he organised 'industrial harvests' with Rolls Royce engines as produce. He also organised concerts at the Cathedral with the celebrity performers of the day including Segovia, Tortelier and Menuhin.

Canon Peter Gould, appointed Master of Music in 1983, re-established an all-male Cathedral Choir and created an accomplished Cathedral Girls' Choir. A Voluntary Choir assists in the support of services. The Cathedral Choirs have featured in television and radio broadcasts.

The Cathedral of the 21st century plays an important role in enriching the spiritual and cultural life of the City and County. In addition to the regular Sunday and week-day services, the Cathedral hosts many special annual services. Examples include the Legal Service for the High Sheriff of Derbyshire, the Bishop's Badge Service, the Festival Eucharist, the services for Graduates of the University of Derby and the Holocaust Memorial Service. At one special service in 2014 to celebrate 175 years of trains in Derby, William Tucker, Lord Lieutenant, rode up the main aisle on a miniature train. Music concerts have returned to All Saints. The Cathedral contributes directly to community welfare through initiatives such as providing *Night Shelter* in the Cathedral for homeless people in Derby. It also organises open seminars on important societal issues.

11: A summary of the history of All Saints

Origins
In the early part of the 10th century the Mercians defeated the Danes at Derby and started to plan a new burh. About 943, as part of this development, King Edmund founded the church that was destined to become the Cathedral Church of All Saints Derby. All Saints was established as a Collegiate Church with seven canons which made it the primary church in the area. It was designated a Royal Free Chapel, accountable only to the King and the Pope, thus it was *free* of the control of the regional Diocese of Coventry and Lichfield. The church was well endowed with about 300 acres of land and property at Little Chester which generated income to be specifically used for the upkeep of the canons.

Power and control
At the beginning of the 12th century, Henry I gifted All Saints to the Dean and Chapter of Lincoln Cathedral. The Dean of Lincoln was granted the title Dean of All Saints Church which was undoubtedly a major asset. This new arrangement removed the independence but All Saints remained ultimately accountable to the King and the Pope and not to the Bishop of Coventry and Lichfield who was not permitted to exercise episcopal control over All Saints. This arrangement caused tension and it was necessary for successive 13th century Plantagenet kings to warn contemporary bishops not to attempt to lever a parish share. The contribution was destined for the King. Bishops were however, permitted to hold ordination services and consider matters of discipline. In the first two years of the 14th century, 200 ordinations were conducted at All Saints.

Dispute with Darley Abbey
In 1252, there was a major dispute with Darley Abbey. The canons of All Saints were unhappy that monks from Darley Abbey assumed the right to offer mass and collect penance at All Saints and yet they refused to contribute any money in return. The canons referred the matter to Pope Innocent IV who asked the Archdeacon of Berkshire to arbitrate. The Archdeacon found in favour of All Saints and set an annual sum to be paid by Darley Abbey.

The mediaeval fabric
We know nothing about the Saxon church buildings but a splendid mediaeval church, most probably 14th century, stood on this site before the buildings that we see today. The mediaeval church was about the same size as the present church (before the extension) with a west tower and a large double-gable roof. The church had a large south porch and the walls featured alternating windows and buttresses. In addition to the high altar, there were five chapel altars and the interior was richly decorated with statues, paintings and inscriptions. The link with Lincoln Cathedral enhanced the importance of All Saints Church and it welcomed national and international visitors.

Chapel of St Mary-on-the-Bridge
At St Mary's Bridge less than half a mile away, the Chapel of St Mary-on-the-Bridge was also built during the 14th century. Early each morning, travellers heading eastwards called in to pray for safe-keeping on their journeys. The chapel residents included a commissioned anchoress, a toll collector and a resident priest.

The Tower
By about 1500, the mediaeval west tower collapsed or was demolished. A new tower was built by the master mason John Otes between 1509 and 1532. The funds for the building of the tower were raised by subscription and by highly organised Church Ales and Cakes events throughout Derbyshire. A clock was installed in the 16th century with an exterior dial sited above the main door and an interior dial as well. There were just five bells in the church tower and the bell ringing loft was immediately above the clock house about the level of the west window. The 16th century clock was replaced by a clock built by George Ashmore in 1733 but this second clock mechanism was short-lived. It was replaced by a new mechanism installed by John Whitehurst in 1745. The current clock was installed in 1927 with new dials in 1964. In 1845, much of the stonework of the buttresses was replaced.

The Dissolution and Queen Mary's intervention
All Saints was severely damaged by the Dissolution during the reign of King Edward VI. In 1549, the College was closed, the five chapel altars were removed and many religious artefacts were destroyed. The lands at Little Chester were sold and the canons dismissed without pay. St Mary-on-the-Bridge was closed about the same time (1547) but All Saints was allowed to survive as a parish church, albeit with no resources.

This dire position was rectified in 1555 when the Catholic Queen Mary put in arrangements to sustain All Saints Church for the long term. The former canons were granted pensions and long term resources put in place for two clerics.

Previously confiscated land and property was given to the bailiffs and burgesses of Derby who were made responsible for appointing the church ministers and maintaining the fabric of the church. All Saints Church therefore remained independent of diocesan control.

The Cavendish family vault

At the beginning of the 17th century Elizabeth, the Countess of Shrewsbury purchased the right from the bailiffs and burgesses, to excavate a family vault beneath St Katharine's Quire. She also had a large monument dedicated to her memory built in the Quire. In the early 19th century, the vault became full and a second vault was created. In 1848 the family decided to open a new vault at Edensor and the vault at All Saints was sealed. In 1973, following the transfer of a few tombs to the first vault, the second vault was converted into St Katharine's Chapel.

The Puritans

During the English Civil War the Puritans gained control of the church and destroyed many 'superstitious' artefacts depicting images. A mediaeval stone font with cover was replaced with a gilded alabaster basin. Through the 17th century, the original bells were recast. In 1677 the number of bells was increased from six to ten and ten years later, the enlarged ring was mounted on a single wooden frame. One bell became cracked and was recast in 1712 before being replaced in 1815.

The rebuilding of the church

During the late 17th century the state of the main church fabric decayed and despite major repairs the condition deteriorated. In 1719 the new minister, the fiery Dr Michael Hutchinson, decided that building a new church was the solution. He was opposed by Derby Corporation and influential parishioners who loved the mediaeval church. Dr Hutchinson wore down the opposition and in February 1722, the task committee recommended rebuilding the church using a design prepared by James Gibbs. The plan did not have approval, there was no quotation and there were no funds, but Dr Hutchinson forced the issue by proceeding with the demolition any way.

Dr Hutchinson energetically raised most of the money needed by subscriptions but the total was short. His plan to sell pew spaces to rich parishioners was deemed unacceptable but an auction of twelve pews did finally take place. All this effort raised £3,500 and a final £500 was raised by selling property. The new church was completed remarkably quickly and it opened in November 1725.

The organs at All Saints

Soon after the church was built, parishioners lamented the absence of an organ. More property was sold and a gallery with an organ loft was built. Then in 1743, a second hand Smith organ (dating from 1703) was installed with its original large classical casing. The organ did not prove reliable and was replaced by a larger Eliot organ in 1808. To reflect Victorian taste, the Eliot organ was replaced by the romantic Stringer organ in 1879. By the 1930s the Stringer organ was considered poor. So in 1939, a Compton organ was purchased. Initially the pipes were just enclosed in boxes but in 1964 it was enclosed by an elegant neo-gothic case designed by Sebastian Comper.

The Victorian quest for a new beauty

During the mid to late 19th century the Victorian taste for beauty in the church was very different from that of early Georgian England. The Victorians wanted to introduce more colour with subdued lighting. The beautiful wrought iron chancel screen was greatly reduced. Three richly coloured stain glass windows were installed in the east wall as a memorial to Prince Albert and the plain glass of the aisle windows was replaced with coloured glass. Outside the church the Robert Bakewell gates and railings were replaced with ornate Victorian railings.

All Saints becomes a Cathedral

In 1884 All Saints Church was moved into the new Diocese of Southwell and a suffragan Bishop of Derby was appointed. Then in 1927 the new Diocese of Derby was created and All Saints was chosen as the Cathedral Church.

The 20th century developments

During the 20th century many of the Victorian changes were reversed. In 1904, the chancel screen was restored and in 1927, the coloured glass of the aisle windows was replaced by plain glass. An easterly extension (completed 1972), designed by Sebastian Comper, brought many benefits. It included an elegant Roman style baldacchino built over the altar and a Retro-Choir located behind the sanctuary. There were also new facilities for clergy, the choir and Chapter and the route for Cathedral processions was much improved. In 2003, HM The Queen opened a Cathedral Centre and she returned in 2010 for the Royal Maundy service. The Cathedral holds a large number of special events each year in support of the City and Council. In 2014, the Cathedral was awarded a major grant to replace the boiler, rewire the building and install new lighting.

11.1   A summary chart of events

900	
917	Queen Aethelflaed defeats the Danes at Derby. She dies the following year.
921 - 945	The new burh of Derby is set out on either side of the north-south spinal road.
About 943	All Saints Church founded as a Royal Free Chapel by King Edmund.

1000	
1086	Domesday Book indicates that the premier church [All Saints] had seven canons.

1100	
1100-1107	All Saints Church is gifted by Henry I to the Dean and Chapter of Lincoln Cathedral.
1154	Henry II formally confirms the gift of All Saints to Lincoln Cathedral.
1161-1170	The Abbey at Darley founded by Hugo of Derby who becomes the first Abbot. He also holds the title Dean of Derby.

1200	
1252	The Canons of All Saints request the intervention of Pope Innocent IV in a dispute with the Darley Abbey concerning the lack of payment for various benefits. The canons of All Saints win the dispute.
1254	Henry III tells the Bishop of Coventry and Lichfield not to collect prebendary income from All Saints Church.
1267	Easter Day: Henry III visits All Saints and appoints Roger (a chaplain) to a long standing vacancy as a canon.
1278	King Edward I confirms that All Saints is a Royal Free Chapel. He grants the Seal.
1285	Roger Longespée, Bishop of Coventry and Lichfield, summoned to the King's Court Winchester to answer charges of contempt of the King and the See of St Peter.
1288	King Edward I warns Bishop Roger Longespée not to interfere at All Saints.
1292	King Edward informs Bishop Roger Longespeé that he does not have the power of Visitor to any free chapel in the diocese.

1300	
1301-1302	On behalf of Bishop Walter de Langton, John Halton, Bishop of Carlisle, ordains 64 sub-deacons, deacons and priests in 1301 and a further 139 clergy in 1302.

1400	
1440	Sub-Dean John Lawe known to be active.
1475	Recorded re-pointing of the old tower. It was dismantled at some date before 1509.

1500	
1509	Building of the new church tower begins.
1520	The date of casting of the Tenor bell which is the oldest in the ring of ten bells.
1532	Completion of the Late Perpendicular style tower. Master Mason John Otes.

1547-1549	Closure of Chapel of St Mary-on-the-Bridge (1547). Dissolution of the Collegiate Church of All Saints (1549). Loss of artefacts.
1555	Queen Mary gives the land and property sold in 1549 to the bailiffs and burgesses of Derby (later Derby Corporation) as part of the advowson in support of All Saints Church.
1556	1st August: Joan Waste, blind and aged 22, is burnt at the stake in Windmill Pit (now Lime Avenue) after refusing to accept the Catholic doctrine of transubstantiation.
1588	25th July: Catholic priests Nicholas Garlick, Robert Simpson and John Ludham are hung, drawn and quartered outside the Chapel of St Mary-on-the-Bridge for their faith.

1600	
1620	Purchase of the Batchelor's Bell (5th bell).
1625	The church pulpit is replaced by a new one which is itself discarded 100 years later.
1631	Richard Crowshaw establishes a fund which will provide £20 each year to pay for a preacher each Friday through the year.
1634	All Saints Consistory Court established.
1635	Installation of Altar Rails to keep 'curious' dogs from approaching the Holy Table. But the rails become proscribed in 1641.
1637	Major repairs to the chancel.
1643-4	New Puritan ordinances lead to increased fanatical destruction. William Dowsing, Parliamentary Visitor of Suffolk delights that he has broken 20 superstitious pictures and removed 30 brazen inscriptions at All Saints Church. Stained glass destroyed in 1645 is replaced at a cost of 16 guineas. Mediaeval font and cover removed and lost.
1662-3	After the Restoration (1660), John Lord and Thomas Willimote, church wardens, appeal to the bishop for help with funds to repair the Chancel. New ornamental font installed.
1666	Bell ringing loft is moved from level of the West Window sill to second storey.
1676	Major repairs involving rebuilding gable end including pillars and aisle windows.
1677	Acquisition of four new bells.
1687	The ten bells are re-hung onto a single wooden frame by George Sorocold.

1700	
1709	15th August: In an invited sermon at All Saints the Tory Dr Henry Sacheverell attacks the displacement of James II in 1688. In 1710, he is impeached but with much popular support is given light sentence. Soon after there is a change to a Tory government.
1713	Church reported to be in a ruinous condition.
1723	18th February: Early morning demolition of the fabric of the mediaeval church.
1725	Dr Michael Hutchinson preaches inaugural sermon in rebuilt church on 21st November.

1728	29th September 1728. After much turmoil, Dr Michael Hutchinson finally resigns his position as minister, two years later than the date indicated in his first letter of resignation. He died at Packington in 1730.
1728-9	Church sells twelve properties and raises £256 towards cost of building a Parish Workhouse in Walker Lane (cost £330).
1731	Church leases 10½ acres of pasture and arable land in south Derby for £240 for 1,000 years to help cover deficit in the accounts for the re-building of the Church.
1731-2	Gallery built with space for an organ. Church sells Angel Inn in Cornmarket and two houses in St Mary's Gate to meet cost.
1732	16th century clock replaced by clock built by George Ashmore at a cost of £8 8s 0d.
1732-4	Spectacular stunts – 'flying' at speed down a rope extending from the top of the tower to St Michael's Church and to St Mary's Gate.
1733	Committee established to purchase an organ by subscription funding.
1735	Serious fire on roof of the tower following repairs on the lead roof. A near disaster.
1743	Installation of a second hand Smith Organ which had originated in 1703. This was the first organ at All Saints for over 200 years.
1745	John Whitehurst installs new clock mechanism which lasts until 1927.
1745	Evening of 5th December: Bonnie Prince Charlie takes Holy Communion at All Saints after his Council decides retreat to Scotland - the turning point in his bid for the throne.
1788	Grand Musical Festival; 1,000 people attend a performance of the Messiah.
1800	
1808	New organ installed by Thomas Eliot of London at a cost of £1,000. Replaces the Smith organ that was installed circa 1743.
1815	The 8th bell, cast in 1632, purchased from William Dobson following the replacement of the ring of bells at Ashbourne Church.
1836	Gas lighting installed in church by Mr Crump at a cost of £26 18s 0d. Ventilation grills made in ceiling of nave.
1837	All Saints sells land in Old Meadows to North Midland Railway Company for £709.
1838	Derby Corporation no longer permitted to hold the advowson for All Saints Church granted by Queen Mary in 1555. It sells the advowson to the Simeon Trust.
1841	Galleries added on both sides of the organ.
1845	Major restoration of stonework of tower.
1863	Three stained glass windows by Clayton Bell are installed in the east wall behind the High Altar as a memorial to Prince Albert.
1873	Major re-ordering of the interior; box pews replaced; central part of Bakewell Screen positioned between first pair of columns; new pulpit placed in central position; marble

	altar replaced by oak altar; stained glass windows installed; John Smith installs new chimes using all 10 bells; outside - the wrought iron gates and railings are replaced by Victorian gate and railings. Cost £6,000.
1879	Stringer organ installed.
1884	All Saints Church becomes part of the new Diocese of Southwell.
c.1891	Eagle Lectern given to the church by the husband of the late Catherine Orme who died on 24th August 1891.
1894	Choir stalls designed by Temple Moore installed; pulpit moved to north side of the Church; new Norman style marble font.
1899	Installation of electric lighting.
1900	
1905	Extensive repairs of exterior stonework. Building encased in scaffolding at a cost of £1,200. Edward Haslam makes new grilles; oak screen panels installed; white marble paving in sanctuary; gilding of pillars and ceiling; total cost £10,000.
1908-1922	Derby Corporation builds an Electricity Supply Station in Full Street which supplies electricity, deafening clanking, hissing and huge amounts of dust for the next 60 years.
1927	The Diocese of Derby is created and All Saints chosen as the Cathedral Church. Central part of chancel screen returned to original position; new gilded reredos and hangings; gilded Corinthian columns and tester designed by Sir Ninian Comper; cathedra purchased in Constantinople.
1927	Cathedral Church hallowed on 27th October and Bishop Edmund Pearce enthroned as the first Bishop of the Diocese on 28th October.
1927	John Smith installs new clock mechanism.
1927-30	Victorian stained glass windows of north and south walls replaced by plain glass.
1930-2	Restoration of the Chapel of St Mary-on-the-Bridge paid for by Haslam family.
1931	The carillon is restored.
1939	Magnificent new organ installed by Compton. 2,800 pipes enclosed in swell boxes to protect them from factory fumes.
1940	25th July: A rope securing a barrage balloon breaks off the NE pinnacle of the tower.
1963	Gothic style organ case designed by Comper fitted in front of the Compton organ.
1964	New clock dials on the west and south sides of the tower.
1965	Installation of two eastward-facing stained glass windows designed by Ceri Richards.
1965-1972	Building of the Cathedral extension and delight as Electricity Supply Station is closed and demolished. Prince Albert Memorial windows and old vestry removed; construction of new vestry, Chapter room, retro-choir and baldacchino. Chancel screen fully restored. Exterior stonework cleaned.

1973	A Cousans choir organ installed in the east end retro-choir to solve sound lag problem.
1974	New font produced to design of James Gibbs. Font located in the Cavendish Area.
1976	John Smith installs automatic electrical clock-winding gear in the Cathedral tower.
1999	Title of Provost changed to Dean of Derby.
2000	
2003	HM The Queen opens the Cathedral Centre; Derby Cathedral Enterprises Ltd launched.
2010	1st April: The Cathedral Church of All Saints hosts the Royal Maundy Service in which HM The Queen distributes Maundy Money to 84 selected senior citizens of Derbyshire.
2011	25th September: The Visit of the Most Revd Dr Rowan Williams, Archbishop of Canterbury.
2014	Cathedral awarded grant of £535,000 to replace wiring, repair heating and for installation of new energy efficient lighting.

Table 11.1 A list of the notable dates and events in the history of the Cathedral Church of All Saints.

11.2 Diocesan Bishops of Derby

Date	Name
1927-1935	Edmund Courtenay Pearce
1935-1959	Alfred Edward John Rawlinson
1959-1969	Geoffrey Francis Allen
1969-1987	Cyril William Johnston Bowles
1988-1995	Peter Spencer Dawes
1995-2005	Jonathan Sansbury Bailey
2005	Alastair Llewellyn John Redfern

11.3 Cathedral Provosts and Deans of Derby

The Dean chairs The Chapter which is the governing body of the Cathedral.

Date	Name
Provosts	
1931-1937	Herbert Ham [Vicar 1927-1931]
1937-1947	Philip Arthur Micklem
1947-1953	Ronald Stanhope More O'Ferrall
1953-1980	Ronald Alfred Beddoes
1981-1997	Benjamin Hugh Lewer
1998-1999	Michael Francis Perham
Deans	
1999-2004	Michael Francis Perham
2005-2007	Martin Kitchen
2008-2010	Jeffrey Charles Cuttell
2010	John Harverd Davies

11.4 The Cathedral Clergy (2015)

Title	Name
The Dean of Derby	The Very Revd Dr John Davies DL
Canon Chancellor	Canon Dr Simon Taylor
Canon Precentor	Canon Chris Moorsom
Canon Missioner	Canon Dr Elizabeth Thomson
University Chaplain	The Revd Adam Dickens
Curate/Minor Canon	The Revd Andrew Trenier

Chairs of the Cathedral Council

The Cathedral Council is an advisory body of appointed and elected members whose remit is to provide the Dean and Chapter with critical help and support. It was established in accordance with the Cathedral Measure 1999.

Date	Name
1999	Sir Richard Morris DL
2003	Sir Henry Every Bt DL
2012	Fiona Cannon DL

11.5 The Organists and Directors of Music

Date	Name
1743	William Denby
1771	Charles Denby [son]
1793	George Christopher Fritche
1835	George Fritche [son]
1857-71	Froude Fritche [grandson of G C Fritche]
1872-77	W J Kempton
1878	Wheeldon
1879	Edward Chadfield
1886	Dr Samuel Corbett
1892	F Bromwich
1894	N B Hibbert
1901	A E Bulmer
1904	T H Bennett
1921-29	Dr A G Claypole
1930	Dr A W Wilcock
1933	G H Heath Gracie
1958	Wallace Michael Ross
1983	Canon Peter David Gould
2015	Hugh Morris

11.6 The Cathedral Ringing Masters

Date	Name
1927-1947	James Paggett
1947-1970	Harold Taylor
1970-1979	David Friend
1979-1983	Michael Fould
1983-1994	Pat Halls
1994	John Heaton

11.7 The Parish Registers

The Parish Registers were kept from 1558 when it was a requirement to record the births, marriages and deaths. However, all the records up to 1590 are written in the same hand and so they are probably a copy of the lost original. Until 1615, the records were written in Latin but the priest of the day questioned the value of a record kept in an unused language and thereafter the Parish Records were kept in English. Until 1738 the scribe often added notes but after that date, the records were entered on standard certificates and records lost this source of enrichment.

Bibliography

View of the Cathedral Church from the south-west showing the 16th century tower and the 18th century body of the church. This photograph was taken in c.1934 and shows the effects of the build-up of grime over 30 years. From Eeles 1934.

Addleshaw G W O & Etchells F (1948) *The architectural setting in Anglican worship.* Published by Faber and Faber Ltd. 288 pages. No ISBN.

Armitage J, Glen D, Hodgson P & Nash H (2012) *The Chapel of St Mary-on-the-Bridge Derby.* Published by The Derby Books Publishing Company Limited. 16 pages. ISBN 978 1 78091 023 9.

Beeson C F C (1971) *English Church Clocks 1280-1850: History and Classification.* Published for the Antiquarian Horological Society. Phillimore. 132 pages. ISBN 0 900592 78 8 [case edition].

Black J W (1931) *Monthly Notes of the Cathedral Church of All Saints, Derby.* Number 89. 28 pages. Printed by Bacon & Hudson, Derby.

Blunt A W F (1927) *The See of Derby: Being a Souvenir of its Foundation.* Edited by Canon A W F Blunt. Published by the Diocesan Committee.

Cox J C (1879) *The Churches of Derbyshire.* Volume IV The Hundred of Morleston and Litchurch and General Supplement. Published by Bemrose & Sons, London and Derby, 570 pages. Chapter on All Saints: pages 69-101.

Cox J C and Hope W H St John (1881) *Chronicles of the Collegiate Church of All Saints Derby.* Illustrations by George Bailey. Published by Bemrose & Sons, London and Derby. Subscription volume limited to 300 copies.

Craven M (2007) *An Illustrated History of Derby* Published by Breedon Books Publishing Company. 288 pages. ISBN 978 1 85983 555 5.

Craven M (2010) *A Century of Derby: Events, Property and Places over the 20th Century.* Sutton Publishing. 121 pages. ISBN 0 7509 4911 8.

Cunningham P (2008) Blind Faith: Joan Waste Derby's Martyr. 80 pages. Published by Pecsaeton Publishing. ISBN 978 0 9556325 3 8.

Curl J S (1999) A Dictionary of Architecture. 833 pages. Oxford University Press ISBN 0 19 280017 5.

D'Arcy J D (2004) The manor and prebendal lands of Little Chester, Derby. *Derbyshire Archaeological Journal,* 124, 285-303.

Derby Cathedral (1972) Derbyshire Countryside Ltd
Derby Cathedral (undated) Official Guide.

Derbyshire County Council (1977) *Life in Bygone Derby,* 28 pages. Printed by Derwent Press Ltd.

Dunkerley S (1988) Robert Bakewell: Artist – Blacksmith. Published by Scarthin Books Cromford. 118 pages. ISBN 0 90775824 X.

Eeles F C (1934) The Cathedral Church of All Saints, Derby. 26 pages. Printed by R B Macmillan Ltd, Derby.

Halls P A M & Dawson G A (1998) *The Church Bells of Derbyshire.* (Three parts) Part One: Aldercar to Duffield. 104 pages. Published by George A Dawson, Loughborough. ISBN 0 9534775 4 8.

Howell J (1910) *A Concise Guide to All Saints Church, Derby.* 16 pages. Printed by Richard Keene, Irongate Derby.

Hutton W (1791) The History of Derby. 320 pages.

Little B (1964) *English Historic Architecture.* Published by B T Batsford Ltd. 256 pages.

Mallender M A (1977) *The Great Church: A Short History of the Cathedral Church of All Saints Derby.* 35 pages. Printed by J M Tatler & Son Ltd, Derby.

Payne C J (1893) *Derby Churches Old and New and Derby's Golgotha.* Published by Frank Murray. 250 copies printed.

Tomkins R & Mallender M A (1973) *Organs and Music Festivals in All Saints, Derby.*

Index

The Cavendish Chapel before its conversion to the Cavendish Area in 1972. From Eeles 1934.

CATHEDRAL
BOOKSHOP& CAFE

DERBY CATHEDRAL BOOKSHOP &CAFÉ

FOOD FOR BODY; MIND and SPIRIT

**Situated in the
Cathedral Centre
opposite the Cathedral.**

The Bookshop specialises in new and second-hand Christian books and also stocks a good range of CDs; Cards; Gifts; and Church Supplies. If we haven't got it, we can usually get it!

The Cafe serves fresh homemade food and a selection of quality leaf teas, real fruit teas and coffees!

**Opening Hours:
Monday to Saturday
9:00am – 5:00pm**

Derby Cathedral Bookshop& Cafe
18 – 19 Iron Gate
Derby
DE1 3GP
Tel. 01332 227660